PLACE NAMES - IN - BOSTON & BEYOND

PLACE NAMES
- IN -
BOSTON
& BEYOND

TONGUE-TWISTED TOWN TALES

AMANDA ROTONDO

Published by The History Press
An imprint of Arcadia Publishing.
Charleston, SC
www.historypress.com

All cartoons by Oseni Ahmed.

First published 2025

Manufactured in the United States

ISBN 9781467158305

Library of Congress Control Number: 2025931727

Notice: The information in this book is true and complete to the best of our knowledge. It is offered without guarantee on the part of the author or The History Press. The author and The History Press disclaim all liability in connection with the use of this book.

To my kids, Abby, Jack and Hannah, who promised to consider cleaning their rooms if I dedicated this book to them.

And to Chris, whose room will never be clean because he shares it with me.

CONTENTS

ACKNOWLEDGMENTS

I want to extend my most sincere and heartfelt thanks to the many people who helped me write this book

Thanks to Chris and Abby, Jack and Hannah for being my biggest cheerleaders. And an extra thanks to Chris for getting those other three cheerleaders out of my hair sometimes so I could actually write. Fadoo.

Thanks to my expert interviewees: Keri DiLeo, world-renowned hyperbolic paraboloid roof expert; Veronica Foley, cancaneuse; and Meredith Yoder, communion wafer critic.

Thanks to Coley Foley III, Kelly Healey and Coley Foley IV for so generously sharing their memories. I hope I did them justice.

Thanks to my Jibber-Jabber friend Cecilia Hermawan for having a great idea and being the ultimate hype woman.

Thanks to the Fab Five: Andrea Dunham, Liz Hubbard and Rebecca Norstrom, and their families, as always, for everything.

Thanks to Amanda Randall-Capobianco, Catherine Harrington, Jessie Tran, Meredith Yoder and Natalie Cusato.

Thanks to my Pi Phis; Ben and Kate Guthro; Mike and Jenn Turner; Andy and Meg Rotondo; Bill and Maureen Hayes; Kelly, Andy, Ben and Lily Mollica; Kurt and Dolores Wiener; and Lauryn Shapiro for always having my back.

Thanks to Courtney Robinson for helping me get my brain back.

Thanks to Mike Kinsella for his willingness to take a chance and for walking me through this whole crazy process.

Thanks to Liz Whitelam and Laura Hatosy for listening and sending me down the right road, and to the WCLC Reading.

Many thanks to the wonderful people who helped me find and research the stories in this book. I didn't realize how many awesome folks I'd meet during this process, and it's been one of my favorite surprises.

- Luann Barretto and John Silva of Christ the King Parish/ Saint Athanasius Church in Reading
- Nora Bigelow, curator of the Peabody Historical Society and Museum
- Dan Breen, trustee of the Somerville Museum
- Trenton Carls, head librarian and archivist of the Cape Ann Museum
- Angeljean Chiaramida, author
- Judy P. Cunniff, archivist at the Chatham Historical Society
- Alexandra Elliott, curator of the Quincy Historical Society
- Wendy Essery, library and archives manager at the Worcester Historical Museum
- Gloria Polizzotti Greis, executive director of the Needham History Center & Museum
- Christine Jesoraldo, curator of the George Peabody Museum
- Nancy Morgan LeBar, collections volunteer at Buttonwoods Museum
- Wayne McCarthy of the Waltham Historical Society
- Max Nosbisch, education manager at the Hingham Historical Society
- Matthew Page of the North Reading Historical and Antiquarian Society

- Mary Porter of the Scituate Historical Society
- Diane Sanabria, archivist at the Leominster Public Library and director-at-large of the Leominster Historical Society
- Ashley Serveiss, archivist for the Woburn Public Library
- Morgan Stutler, assistant curator of the Peabody Historical Society and Museum
- Antoine Trombino-Aponte, museum educator at Buttonwoods Museum
- Brooke Wardrop, vice president of marketing and communications at Zoo New England

INTRODUCTION

Old guys in fussy white wigs waging war and signing treaties is only a small part of history. And honestly, it's kind of the boring part.

The fantastic part of history is the abundance of human stories. A robber baron throws a massive funeral party for a bear. A Victorian guy says we should all live in octagonal houses. Abigail Adams sends eighteenth-century-style saucy letters to John Adams.

As I like to say, "Everybody's just people." And people can be all kinds of things.

They can be brave in the face of terrifying circumstances, act as barrier-shatterers, try to change history and fail, or succeed in changing history without even trying. They can also be giant goofballs, just like you and me.

These are stories from the towns we all love hearing non-Massachusetts folks try to pronounce. The stories that come from these towns are just as varied and quirky and surprising as the towns' names themselves.

I hope you enjoy reading them as much as I enjoyed writing them.

CHAPTER 1

WOBURN

When Ellie from Woburn saw her sunburn, she said, "**WOOO burn**!"

WOBURN PUBLIC LIBRARY

One day you may be driving through Woburn's town center, minding your own business, when you see something out your car window. You unwittingly slam on your brakes, causing a six-car pileup behind you. Your jaw unhinges and drops onto your lap as your eyeballs fly out of their sockets, Looney Tunes style. You sit there, speechless, unsure whether to burst into song or burst into tears, compelled by the beauty within your gaze. You, my friend, have just come upon the Woburn Public Library.

The library was built as a library, which is notable as many gorgeous libraries started their lives as mansions. It was designed in the late 1870s by H.H. Richardson, whose other Boston-area designs include Sever and Austin Halls at Harvard University and the South Street entrance at Arnold Arboretum, though the Woburn library is rightfully considered his greatest work.[1] The money to build the library was bequeathed by Charles Bowers Winn in his will. Winn's family had made their money in the leather

Above: The Woburn Public Library in all its mind-bendingly beautiful glory. *Author's collection.*

Left: The Woburn Library's historical collection includes this eighteenth-century "flip glass." I have to believe playing flip cup with glass cups is certain to end poorly. *Author's collection.*

tanning industry, which was Woburn's main industry and brought the town considerable wealth.

While the outside of the building is stunning, the inside is equally so. A massive wooden barrel-vaulted room is lined with bookshelved balconies accessible by (sadly now closed) wrought iron stairways, all within fourteen semicircular alcoves. An octagonal room furnished with comfy chairs and outfitted with original paintings features a massive stone fireplace at one end and huge windows at the other. It's the kind of library that makes you feel a little bit like you're at Hogwarts and a lot like whatever you're working on is incredibly important.

The original layout also included a ladies' parlor (though I'm not 100 percent sure why ladies needed their own parlor) which is now home to the library's Historical Artifact Room.[2] This mini-museum houses artifacts from precolonial Woburn up through recent history.

Also within the library walls are apartments for a custodian and a head librarian. This is every book nerd's dream (or at least it's *this* book nerd's dream). Getting to live in a building this beautiful would be incredible, let alone a building this beautiful that's filled with books! Pardon me while I swoon.

TEMPERANCE

Ashley Serveiss, archivist for the Woburn Public Library's Glennon Archives, possesses an incredible amount of knowledge about all things Woburn and an infectious energy for sharing that knowledge. During the innumerable hours I've spent researching at the Woburn Public Library, I've noticed that there are a significant number of temperance movement artifacts scattered about. I mean, there are a lot of temperance artifacts out there in general, likely owing to it being relatively recent and a fascinating chapter in history. But Woburn seems to have really doubled down on temperance. I asked Ms. Serveiss why Woburn was a particular hotbed for the movement, and this was her reply:

> *The movement for temperance was a national phenomenon that* [took root] *in Woburn in 1828 with the organization of the Woburn Association for the Promotion of Temperance. By 1833 they had 644 members....Woburn, with its Puritan roots, was an easy place for Temperance to take hold....A number of different temperance associations flourished in town up through the late nineteenth century, affecting local politics. The motto of one group, to "relinquish wholly the use of ardent spirits and all beverages containing it," demonstrates how temperance advocates were in direct opposition to the operation of taverns in town. Woburn had a number of taverns, which were not traditionally just for the enjoyment of alcoholic beverages. For example, Ichabod Parker's Tavern (in the area of present-day Main Street and Mishawum Road) also functioned as a post office and community space to share and receive information. We have a lot of temperance-related artifacts in the archives and museum collection; it is very cool!*[3]

Agreed. The artifacts are so cool, my favorite of which is a banner reading, "We drink clear cold water" which maybe could have used another round of vetting by the PR committee. Another favorite is a ribbon reading, "Cold Water Army"—which, again, seems less appealing than it could have been. I like to think that if I were a temperance campaigner, I could have come up with a better slogan, but it seems to have worked for them, given that they were able to get the Eighteenth Amendment passed, prohibiting the "manufacture, sale, or transportation of intoxicating liquors." This always amazes me. This wasn't a state law that was passed, not even a federal law. It was an *amendment* to the *Constitution*. For context, other amendments established the freedom of speech, the right to a fair trial and the abolition of slavery. This was big-time.

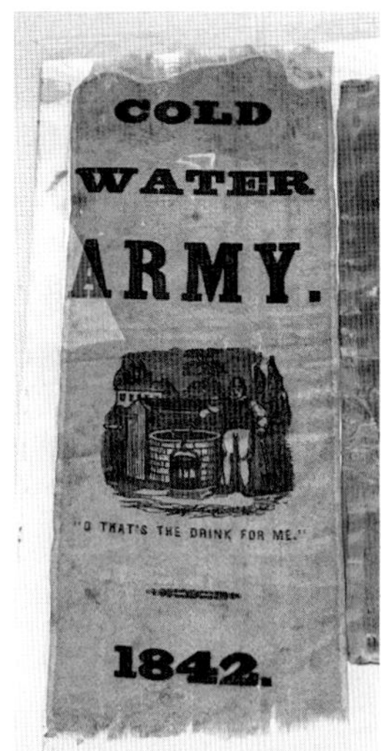

Perhaps the temperance movement would have achieved its aims faster with a better slogan. *Author's collection.*

And seriously, why? What was the big deal? Before doing this research, when I thought of temperance campaigners, I imagined hyper-Puritan rich White women feverishly clutching their pearls over the harmless drunken antics of everyday people. And yes, many of them were just that. But the temperance movement wasn't fueled by a lust for fun-crushing. Much of the momentum it gained came from the utter lack of power women held in society, even in their own homes. In the 1830s, when the movement started congealing, the average American age fifteen and over consumed at least seven gallons of alcohol a year.[4] (For context, in 2021, the average American age twenty-one and over consumed 2.83 gallons.)[5] Women were at the mercy of drunken, abusive husbands, with no reasonable ability to leave. Men could be out drinking all night, spending all the family's money, acting in whatever manner they wanted, and their wives had no recourse. The temperance movement was not just about banning alcohol; it was also about creating a more stable world for women and children. It was an opportunity for women to organize around a cause that was surreptitiously feminist.

One key example of this is the Woman's Christian Temperance Union, or WCTU. Formed in Ohio in 1873, the WCTU first took on, as you might have guessed, the banning of alcohol. In the interest of the public's overall moral betterment, it soon branched out into tackling public health, sanitation, poverty and labor issues. By 1890, the organization had become the largest women's organization in the world. The WCTU actively advocated for both temperance and women's suffrage, arguing that if women could vote, they would be in a better position to support legislation to protect their rights. Through a myriad of measures—many political, some even violent—the WCTU achieved its goal of a constitutional ban on alcohol in January 1919.

When the Eighteenth Amendment passed, it proved to women that, collectively, they could make a huge social and political impact. If women could effect this change without the right to vote, imagine what they could do if women's suffrage passed. Thanks largely to temperance, women were organized and comfortable with the idea of pushing for change. Women won their right to vote in 1920 with the passing of the Nineteenth Amendment.

The provisions of the Eighteenth Amendment didn't last too long. In 1933, Prohibition was repealed with the addition of the Twenty-First Amendment, which I like to think of as the "Hey, ignore that other amendment" amendment. By then, though, women's right to vote gave them some measure of power through which they could advocate for issues relevant to their lives. Other legal measures came into effect over the coming years guaranteeing women the rights that they needed to defend themselves from the types of inequities they fought against through the temperance movement.

So I apologize to the women of the temperance movement for thinking they were just a bunch of party poopers, and I thank them from the bottom of my heart for their work laying the foundation for women to win the right to vote. And if such a movement ever needs to form again, I volunteer to write the slogans for the Woburn chapter. Because with the rise of mocktails, there is no need for another "We drink clear cold water" banner.

---

1. Cultural Landscape Foundation, "H.H. Richardson," https://www.tclf.org.
2. Woburn Public Library, "Library History," https://woburnpubliclibrary.org.
3. Ashley Serveiss, "New Submission from Archives Appointment Request Form," email to the author, April 13, 2024.
4. Prohibition: An Interactive History, "Prohibition: An Interactive History, Presented by the Mob Museum," https://prohibition.themobmuseum.org/.
5. Katherine Schaeffer and Drew DeSilver, "10 Facts About Americans and Alcohol as 'Dry January' Begins," Pew Research Center, January 3, 2024, https://www.pewresearch.org.

CHAPTER 2

READING AND NORTH READING

Reed, who just moved from **Redding**, California, likes reading at the open and airy Reading public library. His friend Red prefers reading at the cozier North Reading library.

Before I dive into the stories in this chapter, let me state that Reading and North Reading are unquestionably two separate towns. I don't want to get mauled by an angry mob the next time I go to the grocery store. They have separate governments, separate personalities and separate zip codes. They are here in the same chapter (II.V means 2.5, for those of you not fluent in Roman numerals) because the premise of this book is wackily pronounced town names, so it only seemed fitting to put them together.

SAINT ATHANASIUS, THE POTATO CHIP CHURCH

When a church is named after an impossible-to-pronounce saint and its roof looks exactly like a colossal replica of a much-loved snack, it's gonna get a nickname. Local lapsed Catholic Meredith Yoder recalls, "Our family always called it the Potato Chip Church, which led to weekly disappointment that the communion wafer didn't taste like a Pringle."[1] In fact, the Pringle shape is officially called a "hyperbolic paraboloid," and the church is officially called Saint Athanasius.

When the church was built in 1960, its roof was the largest hyperbolic paraboloid roof in the Western Hemisphere, and perhaps the world.[2] The architect Daniel F. Tulley was commissioned by the Boston Diocese and given practically free rein in his design of the church. He clearly did not phone it in. As a practicing Catholic himself, Tulley really thought through the design as it pertained to the religion, its traditions and its history. Passersby may look at the church and just think some architect in the '60s went a little nuts. In fact, they wouldn't be the first to think that. When the church was nearly finished, there was a hurricane (which, incidentally, did not damage the structure). Afterward, a woman drove into the parking lot and went up to Tulley with a look of horror on her face, pointed to the roof and said, "Oh my God, did the hurricane do this?"[3] That would be one talented and well-educated hurricane.

Every element of the church's design is intentional. Think about a "traditional" church design: it has tall points in the front and back. Often, in the space above the doors and below the high point, there is a large, stained glass rose window (*rose window* is the term for a big, round stained glass window—it doesn't mean it has roses in it or that it looks like a rose). The overall layout is in the shape of a cross, with the altar and a crucifix at the front of the short, upper part of the cross and the congregation sitting along the long, lower part. The arms of the cross traditionally hold chapels and/or confessionals. Now look at the picture of Saint Athanasius on the opposite page. The highest point of the hyperbolic paraboloid is at the back of the church, where a spire would traditionally be. Inside, under that high point, are the altar and a massive crucifix. Under the second high point and above the doors, there is a set of large stained glass windows. From the high point in the back to the second highest point in the front is a straight line, intersected perpendicularly by the line between the lower left and right peaks of the roof. It's a cross.

Whoa, check out that rad hyperbolic paraboloid! I mean, like, that Gauss curvature is negative at every point! *Author's collection.*

So while the church may at first look like an architectural acid trip, it's absolutely in line with the layout of a traditional Catholic church. St Athanasius himself is strongly associated with the Holy Trinity, as he was apparently a major defender and advocate of the concept. To recognize this, Tulley designed the church with a proliferation of triangles ensconced within the architecture, the stained glass and the altar. Tulley's modern vision created a place to bring millennia-old theology into a contemporary context.

Now, back to that crucifix I mentioned. I know this is supposed to be about the roof, but the crucifix warrants a mention. As an architecture nerd, when I walk into a church, I usually take in the overall look, gawk at the stained glass windows and the woodwork, poke up and down the aisles a bit and then check out the scene up at the altar. The crucifix is usually just a part of the overall visage of the altar area. Not at Saint Athanasius. Tulley recognized that his dramatic design needed a dramatic centerpiece. Always the overachiever, he designed the crucifix himself (and all the furnishings, while he was at it) and had it created by Italo Bernardini, a well-known Italian sculptor.[4] The body of Jesus is eighteen feet tall, and the whole cross must be about forty feet high. It is imposing, to say the least.

Back to the outside, and back to the roof. While the roof looks impressive in pictures, it's even more impressive when you're standing in front of it. Let me be clear: it is huge. Like… vast. Broad. Boundless. Immense. Monumental. Infinite.

The more I thought about it, the less able I was to understand it from a structural perspective. Tulley said, "For a three-inch-thick concrete slab to span 155 feet is extraordinary."[5] Yeah, you ain't kidding man. But seriously, how does this thing stay up? How did they know how to build it? And, most importantly, could I sled down it?

As I descended into my own swampy bog of ignorance, I knew the only hand strong and wise enough to pull me out would be that of Keri DiLeo, vice president and partner at Scalora Consulting Group. Keri has twenty-five years' experience in construction management (which is impressive considering she is only thirty-two years old… *cough*) and has managed the details of constructing what I very astutely refer to as "really big buildings and smallish buildings." I posed my questions to Ms. DiLeo, and she provided such thoughtful, thorough and insightful responses that I have transcribed our exchange in full here, for your optimal edification.

Me: Keri, thanks so much for taking the time to talk to me about hyperbolic paraboloid roofs. My first question centers on my general uncertainty about how this thing stays up. This roof is huge, and I can't understand how it's only three inches thick. At only three inches thick, how does it not get punctured by a falling branch or bird poop?

Keri DiLeo, Only Professional Willing to Entertain These Questions: Well, branches actually do puncture roofs, but thankfully, that is rare. The bird poop risk could be higher. Some of those seagulls, from long range (given the equation force = mass × acceleration), can really pack a punch. I thought until recently that seagulls were the only birds that poop while flying. However, that is not true. Luckily, it is rare for a bird to do their business while they are, well, flying. Because most birds like to sit to poop, bird poop is not a high risk for roof penetration.

Me: While I'm relieved to hear that branch punctures are rare and bird poop damage is unlikely, I am now intrigued by how much you know about the bird poop situation. Is this something covered in civil engineering classes?

Keri DiLeo, Bird Poop Expert: No, I just Googled whether all birds poop while flying.

Me: That's disappointing. Do many of your clients ask about the risks of bird poop?

Keri DiLeo~~, Bird Poop Expert~~: I wish more did.

Me: Another thing that vexes me about the roof is that it apparently required a continuous pour of concrete. Folks who were around for the event recall a huge line of concrete trucks lined up down the street, just cycling in and out of the lot consistently for hours as the roof was poured. I read something about how it had to remain balanced, like a double teeter totter, but I don't really understand why they couldn't just pour some in a balanced way, let it dry, then pour more.

Keri DiLeo, Suddenly All Professional: Well, the reality of concrete is that joints cause weakness. There are ways to pour and seam concrete together, but in order for it to not crack or move at a different rate than its neighbor, it's best to pour it all at once. Another challenge is that concrete creates heat and shrinks when it cures. If you pour too much at once, the heat/shrinkage could cause cracking. Typically, hairline cracks do not impact the strength or performance, as long as the rebar structure is adequate and remains intact.

Me: I thought getting an answer to that question would make me feel better, but all those conflicting factors have just given me more roof anxiety. Thanks. Moving on, this all seems really… hard. Aesthetics aside, is there any benefit to a hyperbolic paraboloid roof?

Keri DiLeo, Appreciates Efficient Drainage: It is difficult, yes. Easy is right angles and straight sides. But from a drainage perspective, this is a very efficient roof form. The other place where we are seeing this form recently is in patio "sails," as a way to bring some visual interest to your yard. You get to enjoy an exquisite geometric form wrapped up with some solid SPF.

Me: So, given the pros and cons, if a client came to you saying, "We want to build the world's biggest hyperbolic paraboloid roof," what would your reaction be?

Keri DiLeo, Loves a Challenge: "Oh. Hell. Yes." I mean, is there any other answer?!

Me: That is the correct answer. So, quick aside, if you were working on a roof like this, would you refer to it in meetings as a hyperbolic paraboloid or as a Pringle?

Keri DiLeo, Smarty Pants: I'd likely call it a hyperbolic paraboloid to those who think they are smarter than me, just to assert my status as the hyperbolic paraboloid expert. When discussing with the layfolks,* I think "Pringle" is much more relatable.

Me: OK, so all the questions up till now have kind of been a ruse to get us to the one question I really care about.

Keri DiLeo, Sees Right Through Me: It's about sledding, isn't it. You know there are railings to keep people from climbing up there, right?

---

* I'm giving her this one as an intended potato chip pun, though I'm relatively sure it wasn't.

Me: Ugh. Yes. Yes, it's about sledding. And yes, I know about the railings. This is just hypothetical. So, how safe would it be to sled down one of the ground-touching slides—I mean, sides? What weight limit would you put on that? How fast do you think you could get going? I have more questions, but let's start there.

Keri DiLeo, Enabler: I mean, it's not like it's a jump. You would hit the ground. If there were a sledding hill like this, I'd do it, and I'm pretty risk-averse. You know who else is risk-averse? Structural engineers! So, that said, weight isn't the biggest concern. Would I bring a group of one hundred of my closest friends up there with me? No—but hypothetically, if I did, I'd encourage them to keep some space, à la COVID social distancing. Roofs are rated/structurally designed to withstand a certain number of pounds per square foot, so if you spread out, you'd be in better shape. Another option is to insist that everyone lay down and only use a barrel roll to move from place to place. How fast could you go? Well, again, we look to physics. What is the surface? Is it EPDM (rubber) or shingles (ouch), and therefore, what is the coefficient of friction? How steep is the roof angle? How much does the sledder weigh? There are really a lot of variables.

Me: I can't tell you how much I love the extensiveness of this answer. Finally, I feel more comfortable with the existence of this roof. Thank you for ending my architectural existential crisis and for teaching me about how most birds prefer to poop sitting down.

Keri DiLeo, Structural/Concrete Psychotherapist: I'm glad to help. And maybe we should try our best to keep this interview off LinkedIn.

Me: No.[6]

If you are a little bit of an architecture buff and come upon a giant concrete sledding hill—I mean, a church with a hyperbolic paraboloid roof—while driving through Reading, I highly suggest you pull into the parking lot and take it in for a minute. It's a striking structure regardless, but once you understand the thinking behind it and the work that went into it, it really becomes extra intriguing. And if the doors happen to be open and you can poke your head in, I recommend that, too. The interior is, in many ways, as striking as the exterior, and the stained glass when the sun streams in is pretty magical.

THE GLORIOUS SAGA OF SAILOR TOM'S

Have you ever had that moment where you learn about something and all you can think is, *How did I possibly not know about this before?* And then maybe even, *How is it possible that everybody doesn't know about this?* And then maybe you have a hard time holding yourself back from running through the streets screaming the story at anyone who will listen, grabbing random passersby and shaking them by the lapels while ranting on about this incredible wonderful magical reality you have just absorbed? If not, you're about to.

Welcome to Sailor Tom's.

This story is so delightfully insane that I honestly thought I was being set up when it was being relayed to me. Like Ashton Kutcher was going to jump out of my kitchen cabinets and scream, "You've been punked!" But I assure you, this story is real—and, almost impossibly, made better by the people who will tell it to you. The next time you're feeling blue, remember this story, and I guarantee a smile will sneak upon your face.

Reading is landlocked. It's in the highly disputed zone of "is it or isn't it the North Shore." It's north, but it's definitely not shore. It's in this context that I want you to close your eyes and imagine… Wait, you can't close your eyes because you have to read. Okay, leave your eyes open and imagine a road through the woods. You're a kid. It's the 1950s, and your parents have thrown you and maybe a sibling or two, seatbeltless, in the back seat of the family Studebaker. You've been in the car for a while because the highways haven't been built yet, so it's Route 28 all the way. Your parents' cigarette smoke trails out the open car windows, and you stick your face into a sunbeam, smiling in anticipation. Then you come upon it. Like an oasis of fun, you spot the animal cages first. Exotic creatures you've only seen in books circle their enclosures. Garden paths wind throughout the cages, dotted by game tents and vendor stalls. It's thirty-six whole acres, and to you it feels like an endless wonderland.

You jump out of the car and bolt for the gates. Your parents yell at you to slow down, but you can't—you have lost all control over your legs. They are going to run, and you are powerless to stop them. You zing past the boring donkeys and take the corner around the boxy restaurant building you know holds a delicious hot dog and a Coke for you later, if you can only behave. Your brain desperately swings between options. What to do first? Go play the "name the animal" game in the zoo area? Check out the miniature fishing village? Climb into the World War II PT boat gift shop to beg your parents for swag?[7]

Coley Foley, a Winchester native now living in Reading, recalls this exact episode from his childhood. He speaks of his childhood visits to Sailor Tom's wistfully, relaying a memory made even more magical by the passage of time. "He was a visionary," Foley says of Sailor Tom, "just like Walt Disney. It was like Disneyland for us, way before Disneyland existed." Visits to Sailor Tom's were a special treat—a full-day trip in a time when the journey took an hour (which surely felt like an eternity to a kid) and led into what was then the middle of nowhere. "Kids go to Disneyland now. I went to Sailor Tom's."[8]

Foley guesses his trips to Sailor Tom's were in the early 1950s. He doesn't recall ever having met Sailor Tom but does remember that "you could see him sauntering around. He was a character—wore a Navy waistcoat and captain's hat."[9]

"Every kid would go to Sailor Tom's," Foley recalls. "No one cared about the ship."[10]

"What ship?" you might ask…

The man who went by "Sailor Tom" was Joseph Thompson, a fifteen-year veteran of the navy.[11] In 1935, he opened a teeny-tiny three-booth restaurant on Route 28 in Reading and named it Sailor Tom's. The restaurant became popular among travelers heading to or from New Hampshire (remember: no highways!) and quickly expanded. By the 1940s, he had added the miniature New England fishing village, complete with waterfalls and a trout pond where customers could borrow a fishing rod to catch their own meal.[12]

In 1941, Sailor Tom, apparently a "go big or go home" kind of guy, had an eighty-five-foot yacht built on the property for his house. It was a true house, with a concrete foundation and zero accommodations for ever going out to sea, but it was built with ship materials, by shipbuilders, and when you were inside, you apparently couldn't have known you weren't on a seaworthy vessel.

The restaurant and attraction closed in 1955. Though the fishing village was dismantled and the zoo animals sent elsewhere, Sailor Tom continued to live in the ship-house until 1961.[13] At that point, the trail on Sailor Tom/Joseph Thompson goes cold. The ship was sold to a series of people, but nobody ever tried to restore it to what it had been. In the 1960s, the new interstate highway system changed the way Americans traveled and killed off the bulk of these roadside attractions (anyone who has seen the animated movie *Cars* knows what I'm talking about), so it's no surprise that the tale of Sailor Tom's ends here.

Or does it?

As I researched this story, I learned that the ship hadn't been torn down in the 1960s. It was still there until around the year 2000.[14] I desperately tried to find anyone who had been to Sailor Tom's, had been inside the ship, could recall any details about any of it—and I kept coming up cold. Eventually I posted to the Reading Community Facebook page. Within a day, I received this message from a woman named Kelly Healey: "Saw your note related to Sailor Tom's. My dad is a history buff and has pics back to the days of Sailor Tom's, and he also lived on the ship in the '90s."

Excuse me? He *lived* on the ship?

I replied to Ms. Healy within about fifteen seconds with a truly psychotic-sounding message. "What? He *lived* on the ship? Like *on it*? Are you serious? Can I talk to him? Oh my God!" Something along those lines.

This is where Coley Foley reenters the story. Not only is he the guy who remembers going to Sailor Tom's as a kid, but he is also the guy who went on to live on the ship for about four years during the 1990s. Kelly Healey is his daughter, and the two of them were kind enough to talk to me about this whole experience.

"It's one of the highlights of my life—I was in another world," Foley, now eighty, said about his time living on the ship. He had been living in Reading with his family when a divorce put him in the position of needing to find a place to live. He knew the ship was empty and peripherally knew the guy who had recently bought it. "I got ahold of him and said, 'Want someone to live there and watch it?' The guy said yes."[15]

Foley, thankfully, is fully aware of how awesome this story is. "I felt I was the captain of something," he said. Though he lived there over thirty years ago, he remembers everything to a photographic extent. "You would walk in and see the stairway going down (a ship's bulkhead). It was beautiful inside; the wood was gorgeous. Still shiny in the '90s. The day they wrecked it, I probably cried." He could describe the ship's three bedrooms and its galley to a tee and was still in awe of how precisely ship-like it was. "They just pretended the boat was a house and made the equipment, woodwork, all to boat standards. They built it with the finest materials; the craftsmanship was amazing. The woodwork/finishes all went to the shape of the boat, not like a squared house." But like a house, "It had a cement foundation and everything. I didn't miss a thing in that boat. I looked everywhere at everything and turned things over 'cause I wanted to know more."[16]

I asked Foley what his favorite memory was of living on the ship. "Coming home from work, parking the car on the street side, walking up the path to the front door and opening it… You'd see the bulkhead and the inside of the boat—I was in heaven."[17]

His daughter Kelly's favorite memory is… slightly different.

"It was November of 1991," Healey recalled, "the night before Thanksgiving, and I asked if I could have a few friends over. Of course, there were no cell phones; it was all word of mouth. Before I knew it, the entire town of Reading—anyone from late '80s Reading High classes on—tons of people showed up. Things got a little out of hand. There was no phone on the ship, so I had to run somewhere and call the cops to break up the party.[18]

"My brother was a sophomore on the football team. He wasn't supposed to play the next day (at the big Thanksgiving Day game), but somehow, he ended up kicking off, and we missed it because we were cleaning up from the party. He was so mad.[19]

"It was the talk of the town. I was in a bad place 'cause my friends were throwing my dad's records off the deck," Healey recalled.[20] Foley laughed, recalling the event: "I think I said, 'It's all right; we'll pick them up tomorrow.'"[21]

I took this opportunity to inform them that my father would have reacted *very* differently and that Healey was lucky to have such a cool dad. "Yeah, he's always been great," she replied. Aw.[22]

Healey also recalls lying up on the ship's deck sunbathing while the whole town drove by. It was surreal, she recalls, and also just plain old fun.

By her own admission, Healey was the responsible older sister. That younger brother I mentioned, the one on the football team? He seems to have done an A+ job of filling the "mischievous little brother" role—so much so that there is apparently a (private) Facebook group titled "I partied on the boat" made up of those involved in Coley Foley Jr.'s escapades.

The younger Coley Foley graduated in '94 and had several parties on the ship, without his sister there to recognize things had gotten out of hand and call the cops. ("Don't talk to me about it! I don't want to know what he did!" Foley Sr. laughingly interjected when Healey started telling stories about her brother.)

Quick aside: I just want to make sure you're really processing this. Imagine: You're a high school kid in a sleepy suburb. Your super cool dad lives on a land-ship that used to be part of an amusement park. You get to have rager parties on a ship in the woods. This is like teenage Valhalla.

Okay, back to Coley Foley Jr.

When I told him that his sister described herself as the responsible one, he replied, "No way."[23] He informed me that she had her share of parties on the boat, and he strongly questioned this whole "responsible one" routine.

This put me in the middle of a sibling spat, and I loved it. I wanted to get them both of the phone and let them hash it out for my own amusement but decided it would be better to let them handle that on their own.

Maybe that Facebook Group is about Healey's parties? We'll never know.

Regardless, Foley Jr. was just as starry-eyed about his memories of living on the boat as were his dad and sister. He described the day he found out his dad had rented the place.

"My dad called and said he needed my help moving. I said, 'Sure, where did you get a place?' He wouldn't tell me. I was maybe fourteen, so he came to pick me up. I asked him again, 'Where are we going?' and he just pulled off to the side of the road in front of the ship. I didn't put the two together and asked him why he was stopping randomly along the road. Then he pointed to the ship and said, 'That's where I'm moving to.' It had always been there—we lived just a street away and we'd always ridden our bikes by it, but I never imagined that someday I'd get to live in it. I couldn't believe it—I was so excited."[24]

Foley Jr. remembers taking some folding director's chairs his dad had and climbing way up to the very top of the ship—"We were like fifteen, so we were agile, like monkeys"—to take in the scene. His friends used to

Foreclosure auction notice from 1991 for Sailor Tom's house, described as a "unique" home—maybe the biggest understatement of the twentieth century. *Courtesy of Coley Foley.*

DAILY TIMES CHRONICLE - WEDNESDAY, OCTOBER 10, 2007

It's been a lovely cruise

A Local Landmark has sailed off into the sunset, as the ultimate 'House' boat, located at 175 Franklin Street in Reading, was torn down last week. Built in 1941 as the residence of Joseph Thompson, the 80-foot long, seven room home looked like an authentic seafaring vessel, complete with a heavy black chain connected to an anchor near the street, a pair of smoke stacks, arched ceilings, porthole openings and teak-board pegged decks. All that is left now is a pile of rubble. The Ship was once Sailor Tom's restaurant and is now just a pile of rubble was taken down to make way for three new homes. (Gino Storey photos)

A sad day for Reading, the Foley family and all ship-kind: the *Daily Times Chronicle*'s October 10, 2007 story on the demolition of Sailor Tom's house. *Courtesy of Coley Foley.*

come over in droves, twenty or thirty kids, and sleep all over the ship, even out on the deck.

One of his favorite memories is sitting out on the deck with his dad during a hurricane. The wind was out of control, and as they watched the storm, a massive pine tree got knocked down right in front of them. Luckily, it didn't hit the ship. The next day, he and his dad got some gauze and some red Hi-C mix. They stained a spot on the gauze red with the mix and wrapped up Foley Jr.'s head so it looked like he'd sustained a gory hurricane injury. Then they drove over to Foley Jr.'s mom's house. "My mom was too smart to fall for that. She just looked at us, said, 'You guys are a couple of jerks' and went on with her business."[25]

"The Reading High class of '94 yearbook has about twenty-five mentions of 'the boat' in the student memories part," Foley Jr says. "My friends and I still talk about it. It was awesome."[26]

The way in which the whole Foley clan lights up when they talk about their time living on the ship is utterly infectious. Talking to them, I found myself beaming, too, just loving being sucked into this world of fun in this wonderfully improbable setting.

"I wish I had a chance to buy it," Foley Sr. muses. "I'd be making quarters all day long. I would've kept the restaurant open, taken care of the grounds, been the same happy sailor that Tom was. You felt like a king when you were in the ship. I was lucky to spend the time there. Whomever bought it was trying to make a buck. They sold the land off in pieces. That memory will never be taken out of my head."[27]

"I enjoyed the living hell out of the place," Foley said.[28]

And I enjoyed the living hell out of hearing about it, Mr. Foley.

EPILOGUE

When talking to the younger Coley Foley, he asked what other story I was telling about Reading. I replied that it was about the roof of Saint Athanasius. His response? "Oh, the potato chip church! I always wanted to sled down that thing." And the world comes full circle.

PART II.V: NORTH READING

Until very recently, the North Reading schools abbreviated "North" as "No" on their school buses, such that there were buses driving around emblazoned with "NO READING SCHOOLS." Additionally, prior to the renumbering of I95, a highway sign offered drivers the chance to go to "Reading" or "No Reading" from a single exit. Which to choose? Sadly, the school buses have been rebranded and the exit has been renamed, taking a large chunk of the fun out of driving around the area.

North Reading is the less populated of the two Readings, and its name used to be spelled North Redding until it was inexplicably formalized into the more confusing spelling. Also inexplicable is the fact that North Reading was a town before Reading. How does that work?

According to Matthew Page of the North Reading Historical and Antiquarian Society, the modern town of Wakefield was the original Reading, while the modern Reading and North Reading were satellite villages of Wakefield (then called Reading). So the name North Reading, given in 1853, is actually older than Reading itself. The modern town of Reading (formerly known as the West Parish) adopted the name Reading after Wakefield relinquished the name South Reading in 1868 and renamed itself after the town's major benefactor/employer at the time: Cyrus Wakefield, the wicker furniture tycoon.[29]

Stories about North Reading were elusive, to say the least. I thought I had a hot tip on a woman named Molly who used to run Ryers, the town store (yes, *the* town store, as in the *only* town store). I fished around and only came up with some reminiscences about how lovely she was, which is lovely. So after a bit more poking around, I started getting vengeful. Like, who are you, North Reading, to keep your secrets from me? I will expose them! I went into the *Boston Globe* archives searching for a salacious event, a murder, business dealings gone vastly awry, a haunted mansion that steals the souls of anyone who sets foot inside—anything I could use to say, "Ha! You tried to keep it from me, but I found it!" Aaaaand nothing. North Reading is currently a really nice town and has, apparently, always been a really nice town. Congratulations, North Reading. You beat Reading to the map, you had hilarious buses and you've made it over 170 years without any major scandal. There's nothing I can do but give you a tip of my hat and a long-distance high five. Nice work.

---

1. Meredith Yoder, interview with the author, May 10, 2024.
2. Christ the King Parish, "Our History," December 11, 2024, https://christthekingreading.org.
3. Christ the King Parish, "The History of St. Athanasius," YouTube, 2020, https://www.youtube.com/watch?v=TvXyo9FgaEo.
4. Ibid.
5. Ibid.
6. Keri DiLeo, interview with the author, June 13, 2024.
7. RCTV Studios, "Sailor Tom's Reading, MA," YouTube, 2008, https://www.youtube.com/watch?v=wET6pRKs_nU.
8. Coley Foley IV, interview with the author, May 12, 2024.
9. Ibid.
10. Ibid.
11. RCTV Studios, "Sailor Tom's Reading, MA," YouTube, 2008, https://www.youtube.com/watch?v=wET6pRKs_nU.

12. Ibid.
13. Ibid.
14. Richard Gutman and Elliott Kaufman, "Sailor Tom's House—Reading MA," *Diner Hotline* (blog), July 10, 2021, https://dinerhotline.wordpress.com.
15. Coley Foley IV, interview with the author, May 12, 2024.
16. Ibid.
17. Ibid.
18. Kelly Healey, interview with the author, May 12, 2024.
19. Ibid.
20. Ibid.
21. Coley Foley IV, interview with the author, May 12, 2024.
22. Kelly Healey, interview with the author, May 12, 2024.
23. Coley Foley V, interview with the author, May 14, 2024.
24. Ibid.
25. Ibid.
26. Ibid.
27. Coley Foley IV, interview with the author, May 12, 2024.
28. Ibid.
29. Matthew Page, interview with the author, March 7, 2024.

CHAPTER 3

STOUGHTON

Captain Lucas was a famous pirate from Stoughton who would **stow ton**s of plundered treasure in his ship's hold.

THE OLD STOUGHTON MUSICAL SOCIETY

Stoughton is home to the longest-performing musical society in the United States, a point of pride that is "accompanied" by a bevy of other musical firsts "of note." (Get it? "Accompanied"? Like a musical accompanist? And "of note"? Like a musical note? Sorry. I'm so, so sorry.) It started with William Billings' Singing School, which opened in town in 1774. The school had forty-nine students, male and female, and was led by—you guessed it—William Billings.[1] Billings is considered the first American choral composer and was one of the Yankee Tunesmiths, craftsmen who published composition books and traveled teaching singing.[2] Billings was very much a part of the birth of an American musical sentiment.

From Billings's school, twenty-five men (just men) formed the Stoughton Musical Society in 1786. It would have been improper for women to be a part of it, as their meetings involved drinking alcohol. When alcohol was banned from meetings in 1844, it was deemed appropriate for women to join.[3] The society grew in number and in popularity (probably because of the admission of women and in spite of the banning of alcohol). In 1893, the group was invited to sing at the Chicago World's Fair. Now numbering one hundred members and including non-vocalist musicians, the group performed two concerts at the fair in the Music Hall. They wore colonial costumes in honor of their home and their history and performed pieces by William Billings, among others.[4]

The Stoughton Musical Society also has the distinction of being one of the two participants in the first singing contest in the United States, in 1790. Samuel Tolman, one of the Stoughton singers in the contest, wrote the following on how the contest came about:

> *With the best intentions to increase the efficiency of their own church service, the ministers reported that they heard better music at Stoughton than any other place. Reports then took to themselves wings, as they do now, and they soon reached the good people of Dorchester, even the singers of the old First Parish, from whose broad limited* [sic] *have sprung so many other churches to bless the land.*
>
> *Confident in their ability and ready to test it, they challenged the Stoughton singers to a trial. The challenge was accepted; a meeting arranged. It was held in a large hall in Dorchester, and, says a narrator who was one of the singers, "The hall was filled with prominent singers, far and near, including many notables from Boston."*[5]

Tolman goes on to say, in the most genteel eighteenth-century manner, that Stoughton whooped Dorchester's butts.[6] First Parish Dorchester is still around, and they still have a chorus. Rematch?

The Stoughton Musical Society was renamed the *Old* Stoughton Musical Society in 1908, which feels a little unnecessary given that no *New* Stoughton Musical Society was then established. It has played and continues to play a significant role in Stoughton and New England history. The Stoughton town seal has a small harp on it in honor of the group. The Pilgrim Monument in Provincetown references the first musical society in the country but gives the wrong year of its founding.[7] This is apparently because of some beef with another music society in town that came along in 1802 and called themselves the Musical Society in Stoughton. Come on. It's so blatant, it reminds me of the "McDowell's" rip-off of McDonald's from the movie *Coming to America*. Referring to the other group, the Old Stoughton Musical Society website states: "One of their last officers, Frank Reynolds, had the original sign board painted over with the incorrect date of 1762 substituted for the date of 1802, bringing great dishonor to him for tampering with an artifact of history. But his dirty deed didn't go unpunished. After years of incorrectly claiming they were the "oldest choral society in America," the Musical Society in Stoughton (MSIS) continued to lose members until it finally dwindled down to only a few and was disbanded in 1982, with its remaining assets given to the Old Stoughton Musical Society, which actually *was* the oldest singing society in town."[8] Gotta love a good ol' New England feud.

The Old Stoughton Musical Society still performs, mostly at the Trinity Episcopal Church in Stoughton. Their current performance schedule can be found on their website.

---

1. Old Stoughton Musical Society, http://oldstoughtonmusicalsociety.org.
2. Wikipedia, "Yankee Tunesmiths," https://www.wikipedia.org.
3. Roger Lee Hall, "'Hallelujah!' America's First Singing Contest," American Music Preservation, July 1, 2024, https://www.americanmusicpreservation.com.
4. Wikipedia, "Stoughton Musical Society," https://www.wikipedia.org.
5. Roger Lee Hall, "'Hallelujah!' America's First Singing Contest," American Music Preservation, July 1, 2024, https://www.americanmusicpreservation.com.
6. Ibid.
7. Ibid.
8. Wikipedia, "Stoughton Musical Society," https://www.wikipedia.org.

CHAPTER 4

LEOMINSTER

The big annual event in Leominster is the Johnny Appleseed Day **Lemon Stir**, where residents compete to see who can mix up a pitcher of lemonade the fastest.

Everyone should be so lucky as to interact with Diane Sanabria, the archivist at the Leominster Public Library and a director at large of the Leominster Historical Society. I want to get a blankie, sit crisscross applesauce at her feet and listen to her tell stories about Leominster all day long. There are so many, and she tells them so well. I'm tempted to just cut and paste her emails into the Leominster chapter (with proper citation, of course; I'm not an animal) but that would be a cop-out, right? Right. So I'll give you two quick stories Diane introduced me to and then one that's just *so* good it warrants more pages.

SHADRACH MINKINS

Shadrach Minkins escaped enslavement in Virginia around 1850, sailed north to Boston and got a job working as a waiter at the Cornell Coffee House and Tavern. There, in February 1851, he would gain the dubious distinction of being the first "fugitive slave" in New England arrested under the recently passed Fugitive Slave Law. The law allowed for the arrest of anyone suspected of having run away from enslavement. The law was widely despised, and Bostonians were not having it. As Minkins was awaiting arraignment, a crowd consisting of both Black and White protesters gathered outside the courthouse. A group of Black men rushed the courthouse, grabbed Minkins and ran with him toward Beacon Hill, the Black community at the time.[1] The authorities, including the man who had been sent from Virginia to capture Minkins, were slack-jawed. Because this was the first implementation of the Fugitive Slave Act, they hadn't known what to expect, and they certainly weren't ready for an ambush.

Theodore Parker, a prominent minister, wrote that it was "the most noble deed done in Boston since the destruction of the tea in 1773."[2] Minkins was moved via the Underground Railroad through Boston, Cambridge and Concord and, eventually, to the home of Frances and Jonathan Drake in Leominster. The Drakes disguised Minkins in women's clothing so he could join them at an antislavery meeting in town. Minkins then moved on through the Underground Railroad, eventually arriving in Canada, where he married, had four children and ran a barbershop until his death in 1875.[3] His time in Leominster with the Drakes must have made an impression on him, as a year later, he set them a beaded purse made by his own hand. The Leominster Historical Society still has the purse today.[4]

Print depicting a "fugitive slave" like Shadrach Minkins. *From the* Anti-Slavery Record *(New York), July 1837.*

PINK FLAMINGOS

Often the world just feels… off. The way you want things to be just isn't the way things are. It's disquieting and screams for resolution. Why can't things just make sense? Then, if you're really lucky, resolution comes swooping in. This time, it's swooping in on pink plastic wings. The man who created the pink lawn flamingo was exactly who you want the man who created the pink lawn flamingo to be. He was wacky, he was irreverent, he was brilliant and he and his wife wore matching outfits every day for thirty-five years. Yes, Donald and Nancy Featherstone would go the fabric shop and buy something they both liked and then Nancy would sew their outfits. She would also buy any flamingo fabric she saw and make matching outfits from it—in total, they amassed forty of them.[5] Doesn't this just all feel so satisfying? Featherstone designed the lawn ornament in 1957 while working for Union Products in Leominster.[6] He called it "Phoenicopterus ruber plasticus," and the authentic ones bear his signature along the side. In the '50s, the now-iconic lawn ornaments were put on display unironically. Folks in the 1950s loved their flamingos. But as time progressed, they descended into the realm of the tacky. Some neighborhoods even went so far as to ban them. Featherstone recalled, in a 2006 interview with NPR's Robert Seigel:

> *We had one* [neighborhood] *up in Chicago that banned them, and one of our customers said, "What can you do for us?" and we produced blue ones to* [get around the ban]*, and then they banned all lawn ornaments. And they got such negative press for that that they eventually dropped it, and everybody could put out what they wanted.*[7]

The flamingos remained relegated to the land of the gauche until the thirtieth anniversary of their creation came around. Featherstone said:

> *Then the…flamingo hit thirty, and there was all sorts of things that surprised me. Birthday parties for the flamingo? Yep, and they'd invite me to go and give a speech or do something equally as ridiculous, and from that point, it built up again, to where it became acceptable kitsch and almost fashionable.*[8]

Donald Featherstone's iconic pink flamingos empower everyday Americans to horrify their pearl-clutching neighbors. *Author's collection.*

Featherstone passed away in 2015, and Union Products, the Leominster company that produced the flamingos, closed in 2006. Thankfully, production was picked up by a Fitchburg company that still manufactures them as of 2024. Phew![9]

The iconic pink lawn flamingo, invented by a total pink lawn flamingo kind of guy, who appreciated his success and who reveled in the ridiculousness of it all: sometimes things just feel so right.

THE FANNYS

The story of Shadrack Minkins inspired you, and the story of Don Featherstone made you smile. Right? Well, here is the story of Frances Howe and Frances Allen, which will both inspire you *and* make you smile. These two women—both nicknamed Fanny and whom I shall refer to collectively as the Fannys—grew up in Leominster in the stuffy, stuffy Victorian era. They were from well-off families, and being young women of means, they were expected to wear pancreas-mashing corsets, look pretty and marry well.

Fanny Allen's family was especially patrician, with a large estate and a lineage stretching back to one of George Washington's bodyguards during the Revolution. She was born in 1843, the oldest of four girls. By many accounts, Fanny Allen was a tomboy, more inclined to running and playing outside than she was to sitting indoors working on her needlepoint. Perhaps because they had no sons or perhaps because they were forward-thinking, her parents allowed her take on the role of her father's "right-hand man" and help run the family properties. She was civic-minded, smart and well-read and loved nature and animals.[10]

Fanny Howe's father was an established businessman, and the family lived well. She was the oldest of four, two sisters and a brother, and studied music extensively, including eight years at the Boston Conservatory. She taught music and Sunday school at the Unitarian Church (seventy-two years in a row!) and was an avid diarist. In fact, she made a journal entry every day of her adult life.[11]

The Fannys were independent souls and not interested in following the typical path of a lady of their day. So what did they do? In the summer of 1872, they hitched a pet horse to a phaeton and went off on an unchaperoned adventure. A phaeton was not the type of carriage you'd imagine using for a two-hundred-mile adventure. It was small and open, with a canopy top to shield riders from sun and rain. Phaetons were generally upper class–style carriages used for gallivanting about or even racing.[12] This was not a Victorian "camper van" but more akin to a two-seater convertible sports car.

The trip raised more than a few eyebrows around town. "We had decided to go, amid the protestations of the towns-people and the remarks of Madam Grundy that it was not proper, and that there were so many tramps it was not prudent for two ladies to take a trip with their horse and carriage along the North Shore."[13] But, undeterred, they loaded up the phaeton "with lunch basket, wraps, books, fancy work and writing materials all at hand."[14] Their trip took them west to begin, up Mount Holyoke, along the Connecticut River and across it by ferry and then up into New Hampshire and back down. It would be the first of many such trips.[15]

Because Fanny Howe was so dedicated to her journaling, there is a meticulous record of their adventures, starting with that first one in 1872 and going through to the last recorded one in 1904. She published select stories in a book she titled *14,000 Miles: A Carriage and Two Women*." The book is saturated with the joy the Fannys felt at the freedom and adventure they experienced. The first journey held the most meaning to them: "A drive across the continent, or even on the other side of the water would seem less of an event to us now than that first carriage journey," Howe recounts.[16] Particular passages show just how much the Fannys loved taking on a challenge. Recounting climbing Mount Monadnock on their first journey, Howe writes:

> *Perhaps we enjoyed it all the more for the repeated protests of the youthful proprietor of the Mountain House, who assured us the feat was impossible, as the heavy showers which we had so much enjoyed in our morning drive had converted the path into a series of cascades. The mists which had entirely concealed the mountain were just breaking away, and we made the ascent in the face of warnings and water, yielding to no obstacles.*[17]

And of a later journey to Canada, Howe recounts:

> *Rowing is the thing to do there, and we had a feast of it, exploring the "Little Rivers" with so many unexpected turns. Then too, of course, we rowed out to take the wake of the big boats, all of which recalled vividly gala times farther up the river, in days before carriage journeys were dreamed of even.*[18]

At one point, friends voiced concern about the rising number of transients causing trouble along roadways. This was a valid safety concern. Instead of postponing that summer's journey, the Fannys instead decided to bring along a revolver.

> *Before another summer, whispers of tramps were heard, and soon they were fully inaugurated, making us tremble and sigh as we thought of the opposition that threatened us. A revolver was suggested, in case we persisted in facing this danger, and finally as go we must, we condensed our baggage*

> *that it might be out of sight, and confidently took the reins, having no fear of anything ahead, so long as our greatest terror—a loaded revolver—was close at hand, not "hidden away in one corner under the seat," but in a little pocket made on purpose, where it could be seized without delay when our game appeared. As we shall not refer to our "companion" again, never having had occasion to use it, we will say here that it is no longer a terror but a sort of chaperone, in whose care we rest secure.*[19]

After seven years of these journeys, the protests from home had stopped, and those who had been reluctant were now happy to hear stories and suggest routes for the next year's voyage.[20] In 1880, the Fannys began submitting columns to the *Boston Evening Transcript* and the *Leominster Daily Enterprise* about their adventures.[21] These columns told of their unheard-of escapades. The Fannys camped in tents outdoors, met miners and tried their hand at collecting specimens, knocked on (recommended) strangers' doors to look for lodging, got caught in thunderstorms, popped in unannounced on friends, hiked, picked and pressed wildflowers—and people were enthralled. "'We shall look for a report of your journey in the *Transcript*,' has been said to us many times."[22]

It had been thirty-two years since their maiden voyage (pun intended) at that point, and though they had matured as people and as travelers, each recount of their annual adventures retained the very same spirit and joy as the first one. We could have known so much more about their experiences, but upon Fanny Howe's death, the executor of her estate burned all her journals. No reason was given, but Diane Sanabria says some researchers believe the "proper" Howe family feared a scandal if the contents got out.[23] It isn't unimaginable that the Fannys were more than just friends, and proof of that could have socially destroyed both of their families. When you read the exuberance in *14,000 Miles*, it's heartbreaking to think of what was lost in the destruction of those journals. Thankfully, we still have *14,000 Miles* and the story of these two brave and pioneering women who scoffed at the social norms of the day and enjoyed a life of freedom and adventure.

---

1. National Park Service, "'Rescued from the Fangs of the Slave Hunter': The Case of Shadrach Minkins," https://www.nps.gov.
2. John J. Miller, "Tea-Partying Like It's 1860," *New York Times*, November 17, 2010, https://archive.nytimes.com.

3. Brendan Wolfe, "Shadrach Minkins (d. 1875)," Encyclopedia Virginia, https://encyclopediavirginia.org.
4. Freedom's Way National Heritage Area, "Frances Drake & Shadrach Minkins," https://freedomsway.org.
5. Alexis C. Madrigal, "The Guy Who Wore the Same Clothes as His Wife for 35 Years Also Designed the Pink Garden Flamingo," *The Atlantic*, May 30, 2013, https://www.theatlantic.com.
6. Anita Balakrishnan, "Creator of Pink Flamingo Dies at 79," USA Today, June 23, 2015, https://www.usatoday.com.
7. NPR, "The Pink Flamingo Era Ends in Massachusetts," October 31, 2006. https://www.npr.org.
8. Ibid.
9. Cado Company "Divisions," https://cadocompany.com.
10. Diane Sanabria, "Insights for History Book?," email to the author, April 5, 2024.
11. Ibid.
12. Wikipedia, "Phaeton (Carriage)," https://www.wikipedia.org.
13. Frances S. Howe, *14000 Miles, a Carriage and Two Women* (Sentinel Printing, 1906), available at https://www.gutenberg.org/ebooks/71527.
14. Ibid.
15. Ibid.
16. Ibid.
17. Ibid.
18. Ibid.
19. Ibid.
20. Ibid.
21. Diane Sanabria, "Insights for History Book?," email to the author, April 5, 2024.
22. Frances S. Howe, *14000 Miles, a Carriage and Two Women* (Sentinel Printing, 1906), available at https://www.gutenberg.org/ebooks/71527.
23. Diane Sanabria, "Insights for History Book?," email to the author, April 5, 2024.

CHAPTER 5

WALTHAM

Hello, my name is Walth. I am learning English in Waltham and am having trouble understanding some verb forms. Why is the proper English "I am"/"Walth is" instead of "I am"/"**Walth am**"?

Yes, Waltham is technically a ham, but I'm giving it its own chapter because I think of it more as a tham than a ham.

A TITANIC PRICE FOR A WALTHAM WATCH

There is no better way to spot a newcomer to the Boston area than by hearing them say "WAL-thum." According to my research on the hams, it really should be pronounced that way. But this is Massachusetts, and "should" doesn't matter. Waltham is home to one of the funniest place name etymologies I've come across. I always assumed that Trapelo Road was named after some landowning Trapelo family I'd never heard of. But Wayne

McCarthy of the Waltham Historical Society informed me otherwise. In an email, he wrote, "Media and some say Tra-PEL-o vs. us old timers refer to it as TRAP-elow. Signs were once popular to indicate that beaver traps were set in the area down near Beaver Brook. The area down by Beaver Brook became known as Trap-elow (for signs reading, 'Traps below')."[1] So there was no Trapelo family. It's a mashup of the warning "traps below." Words are so cool.

Waltham is known as the Watch City, and the moniker is hardly a stretch. Between the years 1850 and 1957, the Waltham Watch Company produced over forty million watches.[2] Prior to then, watchmaking had been a cottage industry, with individual watchmakers plying their trade in small workshops. The industrial revolution of the mid-nineteenth century brought many cottage industries into factory settings, and watchmaking was among them. One of the lynchpins of industrialization was the creation of interchangeable parts. Waltham Watch Company was the first to create the machinery to produce interchangeable parts for watches, speeding up production and driving down cost.[3]

While millions of watches were made in Waltham, only one of them recently broke the record for the highest-priced piece of *Titanic* memorabilia ever sold. *Titanic*, you say? Yes, *the Titanic*—as in the ship. John Jacob Astor was the richest man aboard the *Titanic* and one of the richest in the world. He famously went down with the ship after putting his new wife on a lifeboat. Astor owned a 14K gold Waltham watch, beautifully inscribed with his initials. It was found in his pocket when his body was recovered seven days after the disaster.[4]

The watch was owned by Astor's son Vincent, who restored it and wore it for years. Vincent Astor passed it on to the son of his father's executive secretary. It came up for auction in April 2024 at English auction house Henry Aldridge & Son, which has handled several other big-ticket *Titanic* items. The final sale price for the watch? $1.46 million.[5] The historic sale of the watch forever links Waltham and the Waltham Watch Company with one of the most storied disasters in modern history.

CAROLL SPINNEY

Though Astor's watch may have sold for nearly $1.5 million, there is another product of Waltham that many would argue is worth much more than that. That product is Caroll Spinney, the man behind *Sesame Street* characters Big Bird and Oscar the Grouch. Spinney was born in Waltham on the day after Christmas in 1933. He was transfixed by puppetry when he saw his first puppet show at age five and played with puppets as many kids do. When Spinney graduated high school, he went into the U.S. Air Force, where he started trying his hand at cartoons and comic strips. In 1955, while still in the Air Force, he moved to Las Vegas and landed a gig on TV with the *Rascal Rabbit* show. The Air Force shipped him to Germany shortly after he started, putting his TV career on hold.[6]

In 1960, now out of the air force, Spinney got back on television on *The Bozo Show*. He also did puppet shows. At the 1969 Puppeteers of America Festival, Spinney had a disastrous show. In the "go big or go home" dichotomy, Spinney had gone the "go big" route, and nothing went right. Jim Henson was in the audience and saw that Spinney's crash and burn was due to his trying ambitious experimental techniques. After the show, Henson approached Spinney and said, "I liked what you were *trying* to do."[7] In a 2003 NPR interview, Spinney recalled: "He said, 'Why don't you come down to New York and talk about the Muppets....I have some characters I want to build. One is a tall, funny-looking bird, and the other's going to be this grouchy character who's going to live in a pile of trash in the gutter.'"[8] Maybe Henson's pitch wasn't so suave, but Spinney went for it.

If you put on your X-ray goggles, you'll see Caroll Spinney inside the Big Bird costume. *Courtesy of LBJ Presidential Library (Austin, Texas).*

Spinney went on to spend the next fifty years alternating between being stuffed into an eight-foot-two yellow bird costume and a trash can. He initially played Big Bird like a big, goofy Barney-type character and then switched to playing him more like he was a child. One of the earliest episodes had Big Bird learning the alphabet. This was revolutionary in children's television. Until this point, kids' TV had been pablum with no educational content or intentions. It was clowns running around smashing each other with pies or dogs jumping through hula hoops. The show took off.

In 1971, *Times* critic Jack Gould predicted, "When the Educational Testing Service of Princeton, New Jersey, completes its analysis in the months to come, '*Sesame Street*' may prove to be far more than an unusual television program. On a large scale, the country's reward may be a social document of infinite value in education."[9]

The *New Yorker* reported in 2020 that "for kids who were under six in 1969, watching 'Sesame Street' had a measurable effect on what is known as 'grade for age' status: they entered school at grade level, and, in elementary school, they stayed on grade level, an effect that, [a study by the National Bureau of Economic Research] concluded, 'was particularly pronounced for boys, black, non-Hispanic children, and those living in economically disadvantaged areas.' And it cost only five dollars per kid per year."[10]

In addition to its academic educational value, *Sesame Street* tackled emotional issues that weren't being addressed in any other public forum. Spinney's Big Bird in particular had many episodes where he was dealing with sadness, making mistakes, feeling left out, making friends and all the other things that can make childhood feel hard. Oscar the Grouch dealt with emotions, too, in a much grouchier but equally real way. Oscar the Grouch was relatable to kids because, well, we're all grouchy sometimes. Also, he was exceedingly honest. That honesty resonated with children.

In 1983, Henson, Spinney and the rest of the humans behind *Sesame Street* faced the question of how far to take that tackling of emotional issues. Will Lee, who played the much-loved human character Mr. Hooper, died of cancer. Spinney recalled to the *New Yorker*:

> *"We didn't know what to do.* [We] *thought perhaps he could just retire, move to Florida or something. But then the producers thought that the best thing to do would be to actually deal with death." And in the memorable scene, Big Bird learns that when people die, they never come back. "We were all in tears at the end of the scene and they were totally genuine."*[11]

That episode was remarkable in the way it dealt head-on with a topic that even many parents had a hard time speaking to their kids about. The approach was direct, as it needed to be for children, but tender, honest and supportive. It acknowledged that losing someone is terribly sad and can feel very difficult, but it removed a large layer of fear for many kids watching. It continues to stand out as a prime example of how thoughtfulness and empathy can make difficult topics easier for kids to digest.[12]

Spinney applied this thoughtfulness and empathy to each *Sesame Street* episode he helped create. He retired in 2018 after the show's fiftieth season. On November 8, 2019, New York's mayor declared that day

Caroll Spinney Day in the city. Spinney lived to see that proclamation and passed the following month at age eighty-five.[13] And thanks to him, we all know that it's okay to feel terribly sad about his passing, but we don't have to be afraid.

---

1. Wayne McCarthy, interview with the author, February 25, 2024.
2. Watch Factory (Waltham), "History," https://www.walthamwatchfactory.com.
3. Ibid.
4. Francesca Aton, "Watch Belonging to Titanic's Richest Passenger Sells for Record-Breaking $1.471 M," ARTnews.Com, April 30, 2024, https://www.artnews.com.
5. Derrick Bryson Taylor, "Titanic's Treasures Captivate Collectors, but They'll Need Deep Pockets," *New York Times*, April 26, 2024, https://www.nytimes.com.
6. Wikipedia, "Caroll Spinney," https://www.wikipedia.org.
7. Joe Hennes, "Memories of Caroll Spinney," ToughPigs, December 10, 2019, http://toughpigs.com.
8. NPR, "A Life Inside Big Bird," May 5, 2003, https://www.npr.org.
9. Jill Lepore, "How We Got to Sesame Street," *New Yorker*, May 4, 2020, https://www.newyorker.com.
10. Ibid.
11. Ibid.
12. Joe Hennes, "Memories of Caroll Spinney," ToughPigs, December 10, 2019, http://toughpigs.com.
13. Wikipedia, "Caroll Spinney," https://www.wikipedia.org.

CHAPTER 6

PEABODY

Poor Jack from Peabody, who still can't pronounce the *u* sound, is scared of public bathrooms. Whenever he has to use one, he asks around for a **pee b'ddy**.

Nora Bigelow and Morgan Stutler of the Peabody Historical Society and Museum are fun—fun and knowledgeable, and that's my second favorite combination, right after rich and generous. When I reached out for quirky stories relating to Peabody, they seemed to have an infinite amount. Did you know that there was once a University of Peabody, with no campus, classes, degrees or students? It was the name of a semipro football team. Hilarious. Also, Elmer's glue was invented in Peabody—Elmer's glue, or as preschoolers call it, "snack."[1] There are a ton of wonderful stories about Peabody. I'm going to tell you a story about the catalyst of many of those: the town's namesake, George Peabody. And as it happens, George Peabody was the epitome of that favorite combination of mine: rich and generous.

GEORGE PEABODY, GENEROUS MISER

George Peabody's story is a rags-to-riches one. He was born poor in 1795 in Danvers (which was huge at the time and encompassed the land that's now Peabody—we'll get to that). His father died when he was young, and he had to work in his brother's Newburyport dry goods store to help support his mother and six siblings. When he was twenty-one, the store burned down, and Peabody went to Baltimore to work in a dry goods warehouse. He worked his way up into a partnership and started to learn the ins and outs of finance. I do not understand the ins and outs of finance, so I'll just say he eventually got into business selling international bonds for states to raise money for projects like bridges and roads. He went back and forth to England many times, since all the money was still in Europe at that time. He sold enough bonds to open his own firm in London and moved there permanently. It was the late 1830s, and George Peabody was now rich.[2]

Like many people who grew up poor, Peabody remained unreasonably hardworking and conservative in his spending. He gained a reputation for being frugal—maybe even cheap. "George Peabody was a workaholic who spent little of his fortune on himself. His annual income was $300,000 and he spent about $3,000. A famous Peabody anecdote has him waiting in the rain, waiting for a one-penny bus rather than get[ting] home quicker on the two-penny bus."[3] Peabody had for a time been in a partnership with the Morgan family (think J.P. Morgan), and they thought he was the worst. Morgan family papers recorded one family member calling him a "solitary miser."[4] But the Morgans as a family had been rich forever. They had no idea what it was to be hungry or to have to work to keep a roof over your family's heads. It was easy for them to look at Peabody's behavior and find it off-putting. Because Peabody traveled in circles of rich Londoners, many of whom had centuries of wealth behind them, he was likely seen this way by many. In fact, rumors abounded that he was the inspiration for Charles Dickens's character Ebenezer Scrooge.[5]

Peabody may have been a cheapskate when it came to himself, but he was exceedingly generous when it came to others, especially those in need. "He provided for the livelihoods and education of his siblings, along with their children."[6] Around Baltimore, the name Peabody is unavoidable. He funded a library, an art gallery and a music academy there.[7] Johns Hopkins' Peabody Institute for the performing arts was initially funded by Peabody and continues to bear his name. He also built Peabody Institute libraries in

Vermont, Massachusetts and Washington, D.C., and funded three museums.[8] In addition, he gave staggering amounts of money to better the lives of the poor. This included $3.5 million for Southern elementary education after the Civil War and $2.5 million to construct housing for London's working poor. Because of this commitment to charity, Peabody became known as the "father of modern philanthropy" and is often credited with setting the bar that (many) other superrich people strive to reach.[9]

Also unlike Scrooge, "He had an extensive network of friends and business associates. One of the most coveted invitations in London was to Peabody's annual Fourth of July party."[10] Wait a sec—a Fourth of July party, in London? Yup. Peabody's annual Fourth of July party was a highlight of the summer social scene, despite the day having become a (not British) holiday just eighty years before. Many of his guests could very well have had grandfathers or even fathers who fought against U.S. independence. But when you're holding an invitation to a huge party thrown by a superrich guy, I guess bygones quickly become bygones. The menu for the 1851 Fourth of July concert, ball and supper included six courses made up of three soups, thirteen meat dishes, two fish dishes, three pâtés and about five zillion desserts.[11] Exactly like a Fourth of July party at my house. While he may have skimped in some areas, the man could throw a party.

When the section of the town of Danvers that we now know as Peabody split off in 1868, it was named after—well, you know. George Peabody lived just long enough to see that tribute. He died the following year in London. Queen Victoria gave special permission for him to be given a funeral and a temporary resting place in Westminster Abbey. The British prime minister offered the newest Royal Navy ship to transport Peabody's body back to Danvers-turned-Peabody, where his will stipulated he wanted to be buried. His grave is in Harmony Grove Cemetery, which is in what is now Salem.[12] (Seriously, stop with the town name changes.) Peabody's legacy lives on in the modern expectation that the very rich will engage in significant philanthropic pursuits. And maybe a little bit in Dickens's Scrooge, too.

---

1. Nora Bigelow and Morgan Stutler, "Peabody Ideas," April 1, 2024.
2. Britannica Money, https://www.britannica.com.
3. Nora Bigelow, "Was George Peabody the Inspiration for 'Scrooge'?" Peabody Historical Society, December 22, 2020, https://peabodyhistorical.org.
4. Ibid.

5. Ibid.
6. Ibid.
7. Britannica Money, https://www.britannica.com.
8. Peabody Institute "Giving," https://peabody.jhu.edu.
9. Philanthropy Roundtable, "George Peabody," https://www.philanthropyroundtable.org.
10. Nora Bigelow, "Was George Peabody the Inspiration for 'Scrooge'?" Peabody Historical Society, December 22, 2020, https://peabodyhistorical.org.
11. Henry Voigt, "The Charitable George Peabody," https://www.theamericanmenu.com.
12. Wikipedia, "George Peabody," May 29, 2024, https://wikipedia.org.

CHAPTER 7

COCHITUATE

Addy It from Cochituate was the hottest college basketball recruit, and all the coaches wanted to **coach It** (**ooo, It**).

Cochituate is not technically a town but rather a "census designated place" within the town of Wayland. The name means "swift river" in Algonquin, a reference to the Cochituate Brook, which connects Cochituate Lake to the Sudbury River.[1]

OVER THE RIVER AND THROUGH THE WOODS

What we know today as the Christmas song "Over the River and Through the Woods" was written in Cochituate by Lydia Marie Child in 1844. Except when she wrote it, it was a poem. And "we" were going to grand*father's* house. And it was about Thanksgiving. I think those are all the differences.

The poem first appeared as "The New-England Boy's Song About Thanksgiving Day" in an 1844 book of poetry titled *Flowers for Children*.[2] Over time, it was set to music by an unknown composer, and the holiday morphed from Thanksgiving to Christmas. It's unclear when or why the designated homeowner was changed from grandfather to grandmother, though the house in question is still standing at 114 South Street in Medford (it's a private residence, though, so don't go knocking on the door).[3] The poem was originally twelve verses, six in the standard version and six more in the "long version." I'll put the first three original verses here, just to make sure we're on the same page:

Over the river, and through the wood,
To Grandfather's house we go;
the horse knows the way to carry the sleigh
through the white and drifted snow.

Over the river, and through the wood,
to Grandfather's house away!
We would not stop for doll or top,
for 'tis Thanksgiving Day.

Over the river, and through the wood—
oh, how the wind does blow!
It stings the toes and bites the nose
as over the ground we go.

Lydia Marie Child's most well-known work now might be this nostalgic and heartwarming poem, but in her day, she was known for more radical publications. She was a highly educated woman whose intended career path was teaching. After reading an article about novel writing, she tried her hand at writing and produced a novel that would be published and widely read in Boston literary circles. The book's plot was shocking at the time. A White teenager fell in love with a Native American man but was forbidden to marry him. She ran away from home, married the man and integrated into Native society.[4] The book made her financially independent and a celebrity.[5]

Childs continued to produce both fiction and nonfiction that was considered radical. In fact, she wrote the first antislavery book published in the United States, in 1833. She researched *An Appeal in Favor of That Class of Americans Called Africans* for several years and, in it, called for the immediate abolition of all slavery, with no compensation to the slave owners. The book also advocated for formerly enslaved people to become fully equal members of society, which was an unheard-of proposition. This standpoint earned her many enemies.[6]

When she went on to publish *Flowers for Children*, the compendium in which "The New-England Boy's Song About Thanksgiving Day" appeared, she made the conscious decision to keep her standpoint on slavery out of it both for the purposes of avoiding igniting further furor and also to boost sales. She did sneak in two stories about race, though she avoided making them too overt.[7] Lydia Marie Child is one of those people who, when you learn about her, you can't understand how her name isn't part of the common vernacular. She outspokenly fought for the rights of enslaved people, Native Americans and women, often to her own detriment. She helped move the needle on public sentiment in these areas in an era when the needle had been stuck for a very long time. I'm glad she gave us "Over the River," but I hope that over time, we can extract more from her legacy than just that.

---

1. Wikipedia, "Cochituate, Massachusetts," https://wikipedia.org.
2. Boston Literary History (An Exhibition at the Boston Public Library and Massachusetts Historical Society), "Lydia Maria Child and the Development of Children's Literature," https://www.bostonliteraryhistory.com.
3. Wikipedia, "Grandfather's House," https://wikipedia.org.
4. Rutgers University Press, "Hobomok and Other Writings on Indians," https://www.rutgersuniversitypress.org.
5. Poetry Foundation, "Lydia Maria Child," July 1, 2024, https://www.poetryfoundation.org.
6. Uncle Tom's Cabin & American Culture: A Multi-Media Archive, "Lydia Maria Child's Appeal," University of Virginia, https://utc.iath.virginia.edu/abolitn/childhp.html.
7. Boston Literary History (An Exhibition at the Boston Public Library and Massachusetts Historical Society), "Lydia Maria Child and the Development of Children's Literature," https://www.bostonliteraryhistory.com.

CHAPTER 8
GLOUCESTER

The lobster shell's luster and **gloss stir**s the Gloucester man's heart.

Gloucester. Even now, when I write it, I have to think in phonetics: "Glahhhw… sess… turrr." The incredible history of Gloucester, one of the most famous of the unpronounceables, can—and does—fill multiple books. Its colonial through modern economies were built on the shipbuilding, fishing and whaling industries. Prior to that, Native Americans lived in the area for thousands of years, as evidenced by rich archaeological deposits. Gloucester boasts a colossal list of famous residents and events. Among them, I found two particularly intriguing. One is a developing four-thousand-year-old story about a Native American solar observatory on top of Pole's Hill. The other is about the patriotism, loyalty and bravery of Chinese American Edward Day Cohota, whose story was, sadly, affected by his era's racism against Chinese Americans.

NATIVE AMERICAN OBSERVATORY

A map drawn by a European explorer in 1606 details extensive Pawtucket settlements along the shores of Gloucester, including "dwellings, planted crops, and managed woodlots."[1] In addition to these settlements, there is evidence that what is now Pole's Hill was once used as an astronomical calendar and solar observatory. Boulders there align to mark the summer and winter solstices. Geologists have confirmed that these boulders were intentionally shaped by humans and shimmied onto a sheet of sand-sized rock shards acting like ball bearings, to allow for them to be easily adjusted.[2]

Mary Ellen Lepionka, a former professor of archaeology and Cape Ann historian, has studied and reported on the site and theorizes there are also "representations of the snake, a powerful underworld spirit; spirit animals—turtle, mountain lion, whale; abstract symbols—triangle of healing, numerical tally, standing stones, [and] stone circles" within the bounds of the ancient observatory.[3] The data collected by the Native observers would have been used to designate days for planting, harvesting and various ceremonies. Lepionka and Mark Carlotto, an engineering and imaging expert, have been working to document the observatory in order to get the area recognized by the State of Massachusetts as an archaeological site.[4] Recognizing the significance of the site, the citizens of Gloucester raised funds to purchase Pole's Hill for the city. This action has prevented the area from being developed out of respect to the original architects and so that further research can be conducted.

EDWARD DAY COHOTA

Edward Day Cohota was found in December 1845 by the captain of the ship *Cohota*. There are conflicting accounts of exactly how things unfolded, but it's generally agreed that Cohota and his older brother turned up in a Shanghai port emaciated, abandoned or lost by their parents and near death. Captain Day took the boys on board and gave them food and care. The older brother died on the ship, but the younger boy survived. He took his middle name (Day) from the captain's last name and his last name from the name of the ship (*Cohota*).[5] Presumably, the captain gave him the name Edward. Cohota (the person, not the ship) lived with the captain's family in

Gloucester as an unofficially adopted son and grew up knowing Gloucester as his home.

In 1864, Cohota joined the Massachusetts Volunteer Infantry and fought with the Union army in the Civil War. He was one of an estimated fifty Chinese men and three hundred Pacific Islanders to fight for the Union.[6] Cohota proved himself a brave and competent soldier. At the Battle of Cold Harbor in Virginia, Cohota's head was grazed by a bullet. Despite that, he dragged to safety a fellow soldier who had been shot in the jaw, saving the man's life.[7] After the Civil War, Cohota reenlisted, and he remained an active member of the U.S. Infantry for thirty years. His service took him to the wilds of the Dakota Territories and Nebraska, where he settled and raised six children with his wife, a Norwegian immigrant. There he opened a restaurant, which he ran for many years.[8]

Five years after Cohota retired from the army, tragedy struck his home. His wife died in childbirth with their sixth child, then Cohota became too sick to care for his young family. Either some or all of his children had to be sent to other families (there are conflicting reports).[9] His restaurant burned down, but he rebuilt.[10] During all this time, Cohota was receiving a U.S. military pension and voting in elections as an American citizen. When he applied for Nebraska homestead land in 1912, he was shocked to find out that he was not, in fact, a U.S. Citizen. The application was denied on those grounds and then his appeals for citizenship were denied as well.[11]

The reason was an 1882 law called the Chinese Exclusion Act. It forbade the immigration of Chinese people into the United States and declared them ineligible for U.S. citizenship. This was in response to an influx of Chinese immigrants to the West Coast, causing competition for jobs. Shockingly, the law remained in effect until 1943. It was repealed largely in response to Japanese propaganda seeking to weaken ties between the United States and its then-ally China.[12] By 1943, though, it was too late for Cohota.

When he was around eighty, Cohota made a final trip from Nebraska back to Gloucester. There, he was reunited with his adult children, who appear to have accepted him back into their lives, based on family photos with him included. He also visited with William Low, the soldier he saved on the Cold Harbor battlefield. The two men were the last living members of their regiment.[13]

Cohota lived out the rest of his years at a veterans' home in South Dakota. By all accounts, he remained proud of and loyal to the United States. At the veterans' home, he would regularly stand outside at attention for Reveille and Retreat, even into his '90s. When he died in 1935, he was not a U.S. citizen.

In 2018, Congress awarded a Congressional Gold Medal "collectively, to the Chinese-American Veterans of World War II, in recognition of their dedicated service during World War II." The Congressional Gold Medal Act acknowledges "Chinese Americans served the United States in every conflict since the Civil War" but does not award the Congressional Gold Medal to those veterans. As of 2024, Edward Day Cohota still has not been made a citizen of the United States.

---

1. Ed Becker, "Cape Ann Beacon: Native Americans of Cape Ann," Cape Ann Museum, October 16, 2020, https://www.capeannmuseum.org.
2. Mary Ellen Lepionka, "Wonasquam Village and the Skywatchers," Cape Ann Cosmos, https://www.capeanncosmos.com.
3. Mary Ellen Lepionka, "Pole Hill: A Ceremonial Landscape," Enduring Gloucester, July 18, 2017, https://enduringgloucester.com.
4. Ibid.
5. National Museum of the United States Army, "Edward Day Cohota," https://www.thenmusa.org.
6. Gilder Lehrman Institute of American History, "Edward Day Cohota," https://www.gilderlehrman.org.
7. Ibid.
8. National Park Service, "The Chinese Patriot," https://www.nps.gov.
9. National Museum of the United States Army, "Edward Day Cohota," https://www.thenmusa.org; National Park Service, "The Chinese Patriot," https://www.nps.gov.
10. National Park Service, "The Chinese Patriot," https://www.nps.gov.
11. Gilder Lehrman Institute of American History, "Edward Day Cohota," https://www.gilderlehrman.org.
12. Office of the Historian "Repeal of the Chinese Exclusion Act, 1943," https://history.state.gov.
13. Gilder Lehrman Institute of American History, "Edward Day Cohota," https://www.gilderlehrman.org.

CHAPTER 9

WORCESTER

When Maeve the soup maker from Worcester whined about sore arms, her sister Keeva said, "**Wuss! Stir!**"

THE INCREDIBLE BETHANY VENEY

The life of Bethany Veney is jaw-dropping. As I read about her, there were five or six points where I thought I'd reached the end of her accomplishments, and at each of those points, I considered what I'd already read to represent an incredible life. But it just kept going. Every person should know the story of this indescribably determined woman. Luckily, later in her life, she wrote her autobiography, titled *The Narrative of Bethany Veney: A Slave Woman*. The following story of her life is derived from that book.

Bethany Veney (née Johnson) was born into slavery in Luray, Virginia, in 1815. She had four siblings and lived with them and her mother. She never knew her father. When she was nine years old, her mother died, followed shortly by the death of her enslaver. His death led his enslaved people to be divided among his children, separating Veney from her siblings. This was the first of several family separations Veney was forced to endure.

After living for a time with her new enslaver, Veney married a man named Jerry Fickland from another household, with whom she was very much in love. While their enslavers declared that as long as everyone agreed they were married, they would be considered married, Veney had become deeply religious and refused to consider herself married until a minister was available to perform the ceremony. A traveler came along shortly thereafter, proclaiming himself able to marry them. In Veney's sadly prescient words:

> *I did not want him to make us promise that we would always be true to each other, forsaking all others, as the white people do in their marriage service, because I knew that at any time our masters could compel us to break such a promise.*[1]

Her marriage was as happy as any marriage could be in which both parties are enslaved by different people in different households. They saw each other regularly until Veney received word that something was amiss with Fickland's enslaver. She came to learn that this man had incurred significant debts and his "human property" (horrifyingly, meaning Fickland and other enslaved people) was being held until he could pay back his debts. If the enslaver could not pay his debts, these enslaved people would be sold in order to pay them.

Fickland and the others being held were sold as a parcel to a slave trader who planned to bring them all farther south to be sold. He allowed Fickland to spend one last night with his wife, promising that if Fickland convinced her to come with them, he would buy her and sell them together, so they would not be separated. Luckily, Veney and her husband were too smart to believe that, recognizing that once the slave trader had her, he would sell her for the highest price and not honor his promise. Veney and Fickland hatched a plan that night: Fickland would run away and meet Veney at a given point some days later. They hoped to escape together to the North. Despite Fickland successfully escaping that night, he was later recaptured and presumably sold down south. Once again, Veney was separated from her family.

Months later, Veney gave birth to a baby girl she named Charlotte, after her mother. Perhaps the most quoted passage from her book contains her words on the moment when she first held her baby. Her feelings on what should have been a moment of joy encapsulate the incomprehensible agony of enslavement:

> *My dear white lady, in your pleasant home made joyous by the tender love of husband and children all your own, you can never understand the slave mother's emotions as she clasps her new-born child, and knows that a master's word can at any moment take it from her embrace; and when, as was mine, that child is a girl, and from her own experience she sees its almost certain doom is to minister to the unbridled lust of the slave-owner, and feels that the law holds over her no protecting arm, it is not strange that, rude and uncultured as I was, I felt all this, and would have been glad if we could have died together there and then.*

She and Charlotte were sold together once, and then Veney was tragically sold away from her daughter. The man who bought her lived near where her daughter stayed, but he took Veney to Richmond with the intention of selling her farther south. After having been separated twice from her family, Veney was adamant that no such separation should ever happen again.

> *I had been told by an old negro woman certain tricks that I could resort to, when placed upon the stand, that would be likely to hinder my sale; and when the doctor, who was employed to examine the slaves on such occasions, told me to let him see my tongue, he found it coated and feverish, and, turning from me with a shiver of disgust, said he was obliged to admit that at that moment I was in a very bilious condition. One after another of the crowd felt of my limbs, asked me all manner of questions, to which I replied in the ugliest manner I dared; and when the auctioneer raised his hammer, and cried, "How much do I hear for this woman?" the bids were so low I was ordered down from the stand.*[2]

Because of this, Veney was able to stay near Charlotte in Luray with the McCoys, the family of the man who bought her intending to sell her south. She was able to see Charlotte often. If she had been sold at the Richmond auction, she likely would never have seen her daughter again.

Though still owned by the McCoys, Veney was hired out and allowed to keep whatever she earned over a sum to be paid annually to the McCoys. She married a free man named Frank Veney and had a son with him. (Frank Veney is not mentioned in her autobiography again after this.) With her earnings, she was able to afford rent on a small house, and Veney enjoyed relative freedom with a pass she was given by McCoy, which allowed her to travel.

With this very relative freedom came an opportunity to work for men from Providence, Rhode Island, who were in Virginia on copper-mining business. She and her son moved in with them and cooked and kept house. They were as content as people denied their freedom could be.

Then, out of the blue, history repeated itself. Just like with her first husband, her enslaver's "property" was taken to pay his debts. McCoy had racked up significant gambling debts, and all his enslaved people, including Veney, were to be sold to meet them. This surely meant separation from her son and further separation from her daughter.

Here, Veney's fortunes took a turn for the better. One of the men she had been working for, a Mr. Adams, was able to work out a deal to buy Veney directly from McCoy. The bill of sale read:

> *Received of G.J. Adams seven hundred and seventy-five dollars ($775), it being the purchase of my negro woman Berthena and her child Joe. The right and title to the said negro woman I warrant and defend against any person or persons whatsoever.*
>
> *Given under my hand and seal the 27TH day of December, 1858.*
>
> [SEAL.] *DAVID McCOY. BENJ. F. GRAYSON.*[3]

Veney and Joe went north with the expectation they would return with Adams to resume business at the copper mine. However, political tensions rose between the North and South, making a return impossible. In 1861, the Civil War officially started.

About her arrival in Providence, Veney wrote:

> *A new life had come to me. I was in a land where, by its laws, I had the same right to myself that any other woman had. No jailer could take me to prison, and sell me at auction to the highest bidder. My boy was my own, and no one could take him from me. But I had left behind me every one I had ever known. I did not forget the dreadful hardships I had endured, and yet somehow I did not think of them with half the bitterness with which I had endured them. I was a stranger in a strange land; and it was no wonder, perhaps, that a dreadful loneliness and homesickness came over me.*

That loneliness was made worse when, after three months in Providence, her son Joe died. While her suffering must have been immense, she wrote nothing more than: "This was a great affliction to me."

Veney moved shortly thereafter to Worcester with the Adams family, where she became active in the Park Street Methodist Church community. In this community, she found her Northern "family" and finally felt at home. When the Adamses moved back to Providence, Veney opted to stay in Worcester, where she found work as a laundress and cook.

After the war ended, Veney went back to the South. She writes of returning as a free woman to where she had been enslaved, during a new era when the scourge of enslavement had been eradicated. On that first journey, she brought back to Worcester her now-grown daughter, Charlotte, along with Charlotte's husband and child. Over a total of four return trips, all of which she paid for with her own earnings, she brought back north a total of sixteen relatives. She bought a home in Worcester for herself and one for her daughter, right next door, so they would never be separated again.[4]

By the end of her life, Veney was a highly respected member of the Worcester community and celebrated in both Worcester and her native Luray, Virginia. She remained an unflinching advocate for the betterment of her family and community, and she owned several homes in Worcester.

Veney ends her book:

> *I am now, at seventy-four years of age, the owner and occupant of a small house at 21 Tufts Street, Worcester, Mass. My daughter and family are near me, in an adjoining house, also owned by me. I have three grandchildren living. My back is not so straight nor so strong, my sight is not so clear, nor my limbs so nimble as they once were; but I am still ready and glad to do whatsoever my hand findeth to do, waiting only for the call to "come up higher."*

Veney died in 1915 at age one hundred and is buried at Hope Cemetery in Worcester. Worcester honors her with "Bethany Veney Day" every July 12.[5]

At the end of her book, several area ministers' letters regarding Veney are printed. Perhaps no line among them encapsulates Veney's character better than this:

> *If I am ever so happy as to get to heaven, I shall feel myself honored if I can have a seat so near the throne as Betty Veney.*
>
> *REV. ERASTUS SPAULDING. MILLBURY, Feb. 5, 1889*

A personal note: There is no shortage of details in Veney's story to keep a person up at night pondering how slavery could have been legal and defended in the United States for so long. One that I can't shake is this: the Emancipation Proclamation ended slavery in 1865, meaning people were born into enslavement in the United States up until that year. My father was born in 1935. That means it is extremely possible, in fact even likely, that my own father would have interacted with people who were born enslaved. Slavery feels so far in the past, so foreign. But when seen from this perspective, it's surprisingly recent—terrifyingly recent, when one considers the enslaved years of Bethany Veney.[6]

Thanks to Wendy Essery of the Worcester Historical Museum for bringing Veney's story to my attention.

1. Bethany Veney, *The Narrative of Bethany Veney, a Slave Woman* (Press of Geo. H. Ellis, 1889), https://docsouth.unc.edu/fpn/veney/veney.html.
2. Ibid.
3. Ibid.
4. Ibid.
5. Margaret Lorenz, "Luray Celebrates the Life of Bethany Veney," *Mountain Courier*, June 28, 2023, https://www.themountaincourier.com.
6. The full text of Veney's book can be found at https://docsouth.unc.edu/fpn/veney/veney.html.

CHAPTER 10

SOMERVILLE

Some people in Somerville love summer so much they want to change the city's name to **Summerville**.

Towns in Massachusetts are named in four ways: after another town (usually in England), after a direction (Weston, Southborough, etc.), after a person (Franklin, Washington, etc.) or from a Native American word (Chicopee, Agawam, etc). Somerville is the only town with the distinction of having a plain old made-up name. Why? Because it sounded good, of course. The name was proposed at the first official Somerville town meeting in 1842, just after Somerville separated from Charlestown: new town, new name. Dan Breen, trustee of the Somerville Museum, walked me through the selection process. The contenders for the name included Walford, after an early settler of the area, but that was vetoed. Warren was floated, after a heroic general who died at Bunker Hill, but that also got the thumbs-down. Then a Mr. Miller, an original governing board member, proposed Somerville because it sounded nice. Miller won, and the City of Somerville and its residents have remained delightfully unconstrained by convention ever since.[1]

SARAH ROBINSON, PARTICULARLY AWFUL MURDERER

When the news broke about Lizzie Borden murdering her parents, the buzz was that Lizzie Borden was "the new Sarah Robinson." While the tale of Lizzie Borden has stayed in the public consciousness, Sarah Robinson has nearly disappeared from history. At the time she committed her crimes, however, she achieved celebrity status through newspaper reports on the sordid details of her murderous spree.

Sarah Robinson was an Irish immigrant who came to Boston at age fourteen after the death of both her parents. She and her husband, Moses Robinson, lived in poverty and often had to move to avoid landlords to whom they were in debt.

On August 18, 1887, the *Boston Globe* broke the news that Sarah Robinson of Somerville had been arrested for the death of a man and his two children four years earlier in Cambridge. The man was her husband, and the children were her own. Her husband died first. The paper reported at the time that he became intensely sick suddenly and died within a few hours. Apparently, the thought was that he had been out in the heat too long and then drank too much ice water, causing fatal convulsions. (So basically a fatal brain freeze from chugging ice water? Clearly the Victorian-era medical establishment needed some help.)[2]

Sarah and her three children, having lost her husband's income, moved into a smaller home. Her oldest son got a job with the Cambridge Railroad and made enough for them to scrape by. The middle child was a girl named Elizabeth. She was in perfectly good health, and then within a short window of time, she was dead. Shortly after, the youngest child, a seven-year-old boy Sarah had adopted, became ill and died within a few hours in the same manner as his adoptive sister and father. Though no friends or family expressed suspicion, the undertaker and the attending physician agreed that something wasn't right. They contacted the police, who opened an investigation.[3]

Three weeks after the seven-year-old's death, the police chief had compiled enough evidence to arrest Sarah. When he got to her house to issue the warrant, he found that William, the eldest son, was in extreme pain and near death. Sarah was brought in to the police station. William did die, but this time, the doctor attending him had suspicions, based on William's symptoms and the prior deaths. He took a sample of William's vomit to be analyzed.[4] Indeed, arsenic was discovered in his system, which appropriately explained the symptoms of all the victims. They also learned that Sarah had another daughter who had died shortly after her husband. At this point, she stood accused of murdering five people: her husband and four of her own children.[5]

The police also arrested a man named Thomas Smith as an accomplice. He was a chaplain for the life insurance company that had insured William and had been going to Robinson's house while William was ill. Robinson and Smith were both arraigned the day after the arrest. At the arraignment, Robinson was asked if she pleaded guilty or not guilty to the murder of her son William (the one whom the police had found ill when they arrived to arrest her). She turned to her lawyer, exclaimed, "Is Willie dead?" and then fainted. Because she was removed from the home while William was still alive, she hadn't known his fate until she was asked how she pleaded on charges of his murder.[6]

People who knew both Robinson and Smith were interviewed by the *Globe*, and all were shocked by the allegations. The wife of Sarah Robinson's church pastor spoke at length about how full of grief Robinson had been over the death of her youngest son and how she shed tears nearly every time the two saw each other. The chief of the Hyde Park police said that he'd had business dealings with Thomas Smith and had actually rented out part of his home to him as well. Smith was well established in the Hyde Park community and had a stellar reputation.[7]

Another man interviewed by the *Globe* was outside the courtroom the day of the arraignment. A Cambridge constable, he told a story of being asked to collect a debt Sarah Robinson owed to her landlord. He had dealings with her again after she defaulted on payments for a $100 purchase of furniture. Robinson apparently "mortgaged" the furniture to three different lenders for $400 each and used part of the money to pay off the original debt. Then she paid back the $1,200 all at one time with part of a $3,000 windfall she said she received from an insurance policy left to her by a friend who had died. The constable noted that the whole scenario was extremely shady and gave him a bad impression of Robinson's character.[8]

The constable was right to have a bad impression. The $3,000 was likely stolen from the room of Robinson's potential first victim, a man named Oliver Sleeper. Years prior, Sleeper had been Robinson's elderly landlord, and Robinson had been "taking care of" him when he took sick. (It's unclear whether he fell sick by Robinson's hand or if it happened naturally.)[9] The cause of his death was deemed heart failure, but given that her second victim's death was attributed to drinking too much ice water too fast, it's safe to say determined causes of death weren't terribly reliable at that time.

As police searched for a motive for the murders of her husband and three children, they discovered that Sarah had taken out life insurance policies on her children to the tune of thousands of dollars. She had also received a $2,000 insurance payout when her husband died. And when they searched for a murder weapon, they discovered a large supply of arsenic in Robinson's home. Smith was released without charges when no evidence was found linking him to the crimes.

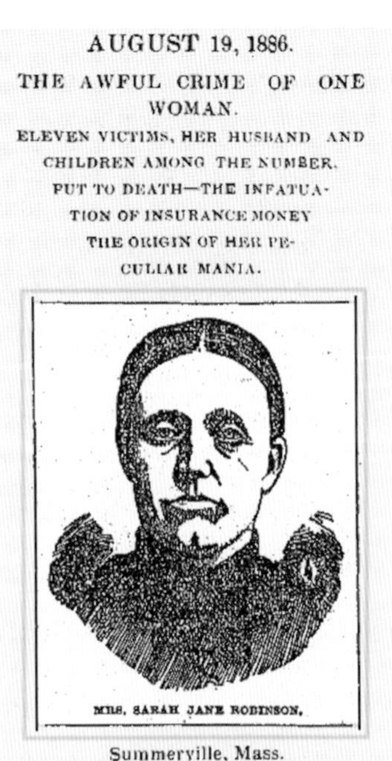

AUGUST 19, 1886.

THE AWFUL CRIME OF ONE WOMAN.

ELEVEN VICTIMS, HER HUSBAND AND CHILDREN AMONG THE NUMBER. PUT TO DEATH—THE INFATUATION OF INSURANCE MONEY THE ORIGIN OF HER PECULIAR MANIA.

MRS. SARAH JANE ROBINSON,

Summerville, Mass.

When you murder eight people, you don't get a flattering picture in the paper. *Courtesy of Murder by Gaslight.*

Media coverage continued in excruciating detail, plastering the front page each day of the five-day trial. This was the O.J. Simpson trial of its day. Over the course of the trial, it came out that Robinson had murdered seven people, almost all of whom were members of her own family: her landlord (1881); her husband (1882); her young daughter Emma (1884); her sister and brother-in-law (1885); and her older daughter Elizabeth, her seven-year-old nephew/adopted son and her son William (1886).

In fact, after she murdered her sister and brother-in-law, she discovered that the beneficiary of their life insurance was their son. She adopted him so that when she then murdered him, she would inherit that money. That got her another $4,000. For very obvious reasons, the people of Boston were disgusted and outraged. Human nature being what it is, they were also intrigued.

The insidious story just kept getting worse. Robinson had encouraged her daughter Elizabeth to take out a life insurance policy, and when she did, she made William (her brother) the beneficiary. When "Lizzie" started talking about getting married, she suddenly got sick and died. The insurance money went to William, who died shortly after the payout. That money then went to Robinson.[10]

Though the story continued to unfold in the press, the trial itself was limited to the murder of William. This meant the prosecutors couldn't mention any of the arsenic deaths besides William's. The trial ended in a hung jury. Robinson's next trial was for the murders of her sister and brother-in-law, their son (who became Robinson's adopted son), her landlord Oliver Sleeper and her husband, Moses Robinson. Robinson was found guilty of first degree murder and sentenced to hang.

Despite the horror of her crimes, there were mixed reactions to the sentence. The *Boston Globe* reported:

> *The feeling in Cambridge over the contents of the rescript as announced in last evening's papers was without much sympathy for the condemned. Strange to say the most determined and unwavering believers in the penalty of hanging are women. Mothers condemn her without pity, and daughters abhor her for the crimes with which she is charged. Married and single, old and young agree that hanging is the only proper punishment for her. On the other hand a large number of the male population believe her guilty of everything charged to her, but at the same time express the belief that the ends of justice will be just as effectually reached by imprisonment for life. Others, and by far the greater number, say that she should hang, her crime being an unusually revolting one.*[11]

Robinson's lawyers appealed the case to the Supreme Court and were denied. Meanwhile, the people opposed to her hanging rallied to keep Sarah Robinson from the gallows. Seven members of the convicting jury and seventy-six ministers were among the five hundred individuals who signed a petition to commute her sentence to life in prison. The petition worked, and Robinson's sentence was commuted to life in solitary confinement. She served nearly eighteen years of that sentence before dying in prison in 1906—*not* of arsenic poisoning.[12]

Given the truly vile nature of the murders and the extent to which modern Americans love true crime stories, it's shocking that so few know about Sarah Robinson. Her story was back-burnered in 1893 when New Bedford's Lizzie Borden captivated people's macabre attention with her murder trial. It seems there is always some salacious new trial that makes the one before it fade away.

---

1. Dan Breen, interview with the author, April 9, 2024.
2. *Boston Globe*, "Is Willie Dead?" August 12, 1886.
3. Ibid.
4. Robert Wilhelm, "The Massachusetts Borgia," *Murder by Gaslight* (blog), March 2, 2013, http://www.murderbygaslight.com.
5. James E. Arsenault & Company, "The Official Report of the Trial of Sarah Jane Robinson for the Murder of Prince Arthur Freeman […]," https://www.jamesarsenault.com.
6. *Boston Globe*, "Is Willie Dead?" August 12, 1886.
7. Ibid.
8. Ibid.
9. Robert Wilhelm, "The Massachusetts Borgia," *Murder by Gaslight* (blog), March 2, 2013, http://www.murderbygaslight.com.
10. Ibid.
11. *Boston Globe*, "Exceptions Overruled," May 4, 1888.
12. Robert Wilhelm, "The Massachusetts Borgia," *Murder by Gaslight* (blog), March 2, 2013, http://www.murderbygaslight.com.

CHAPTER 11

LOWELL

Grayson loved rhyming and making up stories. He often regaled his friends in Lowell with colorful tales like "Silly Lily and Her Flying Filly," "Ben's Hen Is Zen Again" and "**Loll** the Troll Goes for a Stroll."

Lowell snuck up on me. I hadn't thought of it as being pronounced strangely until my daughter, reading a highway sign, asked if we were going to LOW-ell. She would have nailed it if she'd tried to say it that way but with a mouth full of golf balls. You can properly pronounce *Lowell* without moving your jaw or lips at all. And keep it to one syllable, please. Lowell is the seat of the industrial revolution in the United States. People have to get to work—nobody has time for more than one syllable.

If there is one thing to know about Lowell, it's mills. The city is a patchwork of huge brick nineteenth-century mill buildings that fell into disrepair as the mills closed over the decades due to manufacturing shifting overseas. Until the early 2000s, many of them were abandoned, graffiti-covered and in decay. Now, most if not all have been converted into offices or housing, leveraging the high ceilings, brickwork and huge windows. A lively restaurant and arts scene has popped up, and the city is alive again.

While Lowell is most known for its mills, the city contains tons of other fascinating history. Bette Davis was born there, as was Jack Kerouac (who is also buried there). The Middlesex Canal, an engineering marvel of its time and the predecessor to the way-more-famous-with-its-showoff-song Erie Canal, ran through Lowell and provided a quick and relatively cheap means of transportation for people and goods to and from Boston. It had an impressive early streetcar system and a robust turn-of-the-century cultural scene. Lowell was home to a strong antislavery movement and the site of several stops on the Underground Railroad. Woven* in among all this are, of course, fascinating stories of fascinating people. The city seems to have a knack for producing incredibly accomplished individuals who unapologetically blow right past social and cultural conventions that seek to hold them back. There are few things more admirable or more able to change the world.

Bucky Lew, Basketball Pioneer

One of these people is Bucky Lew. Lew was a star player in the nascent New England Basketball League as part of the Lowell-Pawtucketville Athletic Club. This was in 1902, and basketball had just been invented eleven years earlier in 1891. So when I say "nascent," I mean super new. Like if basketball were a person, it wouldn't even have been old enough to gets its driver's license.

Harry Haskell Lew, better known as Bucky, was born in 1884 into a prominent Black family. He was an accomplished musician, as were many members of his family. In fact, his great-great-grandfather Barzillai, a freeman, had been a fifer in the Revolutionary War at the Battle of Bunker Hill. His father ran a successful dry cleaning company and was a delegate to the 1891 Equal Rights Convention in Boston. His two sisters were the first Black people (women *or* men) to graduate from UMass Lowell (known then as the Lowell Normal School), and one went on to become the first Black

* Mill pun.

teacher in Lowell's public schools and the first Black person to graduate from what is now New England School of Law. His brother founded the first Black history and culture museum in the country. The Lews were one impressive family.[1]

Lew started playing basketball at age fourteen with a local YMCA team and gained a reputation for agility and speed. While he did score what were considered "big points" at the time, he really excelled in defensive positions and was noted for his ability to hold off one of the biggest scorers of the time, Harry Hough. I am wildly deficient in my knowledge of the game of basketball, so I will spare us all the embarrassment of me trying to speak to Lew's technical prowess. A new biography (the first of Lew), *The Original Bucky Lew: Basketball's First Black Professional*, by Lowell native Chris Boucher, does, however, succeed in covering that part of the story (as well as the rest of it) for any of you sports-y types.[2]

Bucky Lew, the first Black professional basketball player, and his formidable-looking teammates. *Courtesy of African American Registry.*

As a non-sportsy type, the best part of the Lew story for me is how supportive the Lowell-Pawtucketville fans were of him. Turn-of-the-century America was not exactly an integrated utopia, so it wouldn't have been surprising if the team's fans were not thrilled about having the league's only Black player. In this 1958 interview with the now-defunct *Springfield Union* newspaper, Lew spoke about the first professional game he played, against a team from Marlborough, Massachusetts, after having been kept off the court for the first games of the season by the team's manager:

> *I can almost see the faces of those Marlborough players when I got into that game. Our Lowell team had been getting players from New York, New Jersey, Pennsylvania, and some of the local papers put the pressure on by demanding that they give this little Negro from around the corner a chance to play. Well, at first, the team just ignored the publicity. But a series of injuries forced the manager to take me on for the Marlborough game. I made the sixth player that night, and he said all I had to do was sit on the bench for my five bucks pay.*
>
> *It just so happens that one of the Lowell players got himself injured and had to leave the game. At first, this manager refused to put me in. He let them play us five on four, but the fans got mad and almost started a riot, screaming to let me play. That did it. I went in there, and you know…all those things you read about Jackie Robinson, the abuse, the name-calling, extra effort to put him down…they're all true. I got the same treatment, and even worse. Basketball was a rough game then. I took the bumps, the elbows in the gut, knees here, and everything else that went with it. But I gave it right back. It was rough but worth it.*
>
> *Once they knew I could take it, I had it made. Some of those same boys who gave the hardest licks turned out to be among my best friends in the years that followed.*[3]

The New England Basketball League only lasted four seasons, until 1905. At that point, Lew joined another short-lived league and then went on to form a barnstorming team (think proto–Harlem Globetrotters) called Bucky Lew's Traveling Five that traveled New England for over twenty-five years.[4] He became the first Black coach of an integrated college team in 1922 when he took a coaching job at what is now UMass Lowell.[5] For context, the NBA color barrier wouldn't be broken until 1950, when Chuck Cooper was drafted by the Boston Celtics. Lew eventually left the basketball world in his forties and moved his dry-cleaning business from Lowell to Springfield, where he lived and raised a family.

Shockingly, though he is recognized as the first Black professional basketball player, Bucky Lew is not an inductee of or mentioned anywhere in the Basketball Hall of Fame. There are some reasons swirling around the position he played, the status of the league and other technicalities, but his family and several others have been petitioning to get him inducted (or at least mentioned) in spite of that.[6] It seems only fitting for a man who broke two color barriers and who, by all accounts, positively promoted the game in Massachusetts and beyond.

FLORENCE LUSCOMB, PERENNIAL ACTIVIST

In the late 1890s, a class of seventy Radcliffe students received an assignment to write an opinion paper on women's suffrage. To clarify: Radcliffe is a women's college. So that's seventy *women* who wrote papers—seventy highly educated women. Of those, only two wrote in favor of women's suffrage. That means sixty-eight of them, 97 percent, wrote in opposition to giving themselves the right to vote.[7] This is beyond mind-boggling (and depressing) to me. What is even more mind-boggling (and inspiring) is that suffragists were then able to turn the tide of public opinion and get the Nineteenth Amendment passed just over 20 years later. Among the women crucial to that effort was Florence Luscomb.

Born in Lowell in 1887 to a soon-to-be absentee father and a mother who was a force in her own right, Florence Luscomb led a life of absolute advocacy. Though her social and financial position would have allowed her to lead a life of leisure, she chose no such path and instead fought for endless causes over her ninety-eight-year-long life. It requires mental gymnastics to imagine one person staying relevant as an activist through such a broad time span—1887 to 1985—that covered so many social and political revolutions. For her whole life, Luscomb had seemingly endless energy and passion to drive the reforms she saw as necessary to a just society.[8]

To have achieved all she did, Luscomb had to have started young. Her mother, Hannah Skinner (Knox) Luscomb (hereafter referred to as HSL, which is how she referred to herself), saw to that. HSL was a divorced woman in the late 1800s, which was rare and often scandalous. When Florence was young, HSL left her husband and took her daughter to live in Boston, where they lived comfortably off money HSL inherited from her grandmother. When she was just five years old, Florence went with HSL to hear Susan B. Anthony speak. She would recall it many times as formative—she didn't remember exactly what Anthony said, but she remembered Anthony made an impression.

It must have been a heck of an impression.

Luscomb attended a swanky private secondary school, and when she saw that many of her male classmates were applying to MIT, she decided she would as well. She was accepted and, in 1909, became one of the first women to graduate from MIT with an architecture degree. There were 1,200 students in her class at MIT and a total of twelve women.[9] For those of you without the math skills to get into MIT, that's a grand total of 1 percent women. A 2020 *MIT Technology Review* article on Luscomb states, "When a male student released a mouse under her seat in a lecture, she calmly pronounced it a nice-looking mouse. Nor was she fazed by the inhospitable reception MIT gave to suffrage activism. "Any notices of the suffrage meetings put up on the bulletin boards were immediately torn down," she would later recount."[10]

Luscomb and other MIT women took to suffrage campaigning with great gusto, leveraging their energies to spread the word through open-air speeches to whatever crowd might gather. Keep in mind that at the time, women's suffrage was hardly universally supported, and Luscomb and her co-speakers likely faced hostile crowds on the streets. Undeterred, they pressed on.

Fascinatingly, it was somehow socially acceptable at the time for women to give lectures or speeches indoors but not outdoors. I've racked my brain to try to figure out why this may have been the case. Could speaking outdoors have been viewed as "making a scene"? Maybe it was seen as unladylike to project one's voice as loudly as one would need to successfully address an outdoor crowd? Perhaps there was concern about the sun marring a lady's perfectly pallid skin? Regardless, Luscomb and her fellow speakers must have found these restrictions as absurd as they sound today, for they outright ignored them and got their message out to as many people as they could, however and wherever they could.

While still a student, Luscomb volunteered to speak in rural towns on trolley tours sponsored by local women's suffrage groups. Wherever the trolley would stop, she'd disembark and deliver an impassioned speech while standing on top of a Moxie box borrowed from the nearest drugstore. "Fellow suffragist Katharine Dexter McCormick, [MIT] Class of 1904, also took part in such trolley tours. Over two months in 1908, McCormick and other members of the Massachusetts Woman Suffrage Association (MWSA) visited three towns a day, speaking 97 times to a total of about 25,000 people."[11]

Luscomb was thirty-three when she was allowed to vote for the first time. That victory hardly stopped her, though. The ensuing list of causes she fought for reads like the lyrics of Billy Joel's "We Didn't Start the Fire." Luscomb was there for everything, fighting for the rights of the disenfranchised. She advocated for prison reform, rights for the "insane" and equal pay. She was active in workers' rights campaigns and many pro-peace efforts, including protesting the Vietnam War. During the McCarthy era, she was accused of being a communist and brought before the Massachusetts State Commission on Communism (MSCC), the state-level version of the now-infamous House Committee on Un-American Activities. Though she was not a member of the communist party, she spoke out against the McCarthyite investigations as undemocratic and successfully sued the MSCC for violating her constitutional rights. She fought against racism and the proliferation of nuclear weapons and was active in the second-wave feminist movement of the 1970s.[12]

A 1976 *Boston Globe* article profiled Luscomb, titling her "Boston's oldest protester." At eighty-nine years old, Luscomb was living in a communal space in Cambridge with much younger housemates, saying she liked living with young people because they kept her current.[13]

From fighting for women's right to vote to pushing for the ratification of the Equal Rights Amendment, Florence Luscomb's activism career unfolds like an evolutionary map of the feminist movement. Her other causes outline the social and political progression of the United States from the Industrial Revolution through to the modern age.

From her hometown of Lowell, Luscomb's journey through life empowered countless people. Despite her no longer being among us, the echoes of her work and accomplishments continue to better the lives of countless more.

JOSEPH CINQUEZ OF THE *AMISTAD*

In 1839, fifty-three African men being brought by ship to be sold into slavery organized themselves—despite speaking different languages and being under the watch of the crew—picked the locks on their shackles and overtook the ship. They attempted to get the crew to sail the ship back to Africa, but the crew effectively navigated north instead, landing them on Long Island in New York. The fifty-three Africans were put on trial for mutiny, piracy and murder, leading to an episode that shows how dedicated the American people were to defending the human rights granted in the relatively new Constitution.[14]

The name of the ship was the *Amistad*, which means "friendship" in Spanish. While that name is deeply perverse for a slave ship, the moniker "friendship" does eventually play a non-ironic role in the story. Among the people who brought true friendship into the story are the people of Lowell.

Joseph Cinquez (also spelled Cinque) was the heir to a tribal leadership role in Africa but was taken captive and sold by another African when he decided Cinquez was taking too long to pay a debt.[15] He was pushed into the complicated and tortuous slave-trading system and transported across the ocean, eventually arriving in Cuba, where he was sold to two traders named Ruiz and Montes. It was while sailing with Ruiz and Montes between two ports in Cuba that Cinquez led the revolt and took control of the *Amistad*.

When the Africans aboard the *Amistad* arrived in Long Island, abolitionists mobilized to get them released and returned home. Lewis Tappan, a noted abolitionist of the time, formed a committee to support Cinquez and the other Africans. Of his first meeting with Cinquez, Tappan wrote:

> *He is with several savage-looking fellows, black and white, who are in jail on various charges. Visitors are not allowed to enter this stronghold of the jail, and the inmates can only be seen and conversed with through the aperture of the door.*
>
> *Towards evening, we made a visit to Shidquau* [sic] *and conversed with him a considerable time. He drew his hand across his throat, as his room mates said he had done frequently before, and asked whether the people here intended to kill him.*
>
> *He was assured that probably no harm would happen to him—that we were his friends—and that he would be sent across the ocean towards the rising sun, home to his friends.*
>
> *His countenance immediately lost the anxious and distressed expression it had before, and beamed with joy. He says he was born about two days traveling from the ocean; that he purchased some goods, and being able to pay for only two-thirds of the amount, he was seized by the traders, his own countrymen, and sold to King Sharka for the remaining third.*[16]

Portrait of Joseph Cinquez, commissioned by the New York *Sun* for the August 31, 1839 edition. The text begins, "Joseph Cinquez, the brave Congolese Chief, who prefers death to slavery..." *Courtesy of Library of Congress.*

Thanks to Tappan and his committee, Cinquez and the other Africans entered the U.S. court system with significant help. After some back-and-forth regarding jurisdiction in the case against the Africans and two years' worth of appeals and challenges up the ladder of the court system, the case was brought before the U.S. Supreme Court. Much of the case came down to whether these people were the property of the (legal) Spanish slave trade or if they had been born free men and kidnapped. The Africans were represented by John Quincy Adams (yes, *that* John Quincy Adams), who lived up to his reputation and won the case. The "mutineers" of the *Amistad* were ordered freed immediately.

Once freed, it took nearly nine months before they could be sent back to Africa with a group of missionaries. During that time, Cinquez and his remaining "co-mutineers" (eighteen of the original group died either at sea or awaiting trial) spent time with these missionaries, learning English and the ways of Christianity. Also during that time, they traveled locally, raising funds for their voyage home and for a mission to be established when the ship arrived. One of the places they visited was Lowell.[17]

The following is an excerpt from *Visit to the United States in 1841*, by Joseph Sturge:

> *In the evening at Lowell, the large Methodist Church, St. Paul's, was crowded, one thousand five hundred people being present, it was said, and many hundreds unable to get admission. The meeting was opened with an appropriate prayer by Rev. Luther Lee. In order to give an opportunity to the audience to see and hear Cinque, he was invited into the pulpit, where he made an energetic address. One hundred and six dollars were collected.*
>
> *At the close of the services, nearly the whole congregation came forward and took the Mendians by the hand, with kind words and many presents. The ministers of all denominations attended the meeting, with many of the most respectable citizens.*
>
> *During the day the Africans were invited to visit the "Boott Corporation," and were conducted over the whole establishment (cotton mills,) by the agent, Mr. French. As might be supposed, they were astonished beyond measure. After inspecting the machinery, the fabrics, and the great wheel, one of them turned to me and said, "Did man make this?" On receiving a reply, he said, "He no live now—he live a great while ago."*
>
> *Afterwards they visited the carpet factory and expressed great delight at the beauty and excellence of the carpets and rugs. Cinque wished to purchase a miniature hearth rug, but the agent allowed him to select one of the large and beautiful rugs to take to Mendi, which he generously presented to him. The workmen here—chiefly Englishmen—made a collection of fifty-eight dollars and fifty cents on the spot and presented it to the Mendi Fund.*[18]

The kindness of the people of Lowell is palpable in this account. The $106 collected at the church gathering amounts to nearly $4,000 in today's dollars, and I enjoy imagining a church packed with 1,500 people and hundreds more trying to get in to hear Cinquez speak. Clearly, the *Amistad* survivors were shown great respect, given a tour of the cotton mill, where Mr. Sturge appeared delighted at one man's amazement, and presented with a large run for Cinquez to take home. The impromptu collection by the workers at the carpet factory amounts to nearly $2,000 in today's dollars. Clearly, the people of Lowell recognized the determination, resolve and intelligence needed to achieve what the *Amistad* Africans achieved and were eager to support them with their time and their hard-earned dollars.

The thirty-five survivors of the *Amistad* ordeal left the United States for Africa in November 1841. The missionaries established themselves in Sierra Leone, and most of the *Amistad* Africans scattered, presumably to find their way back to their respective homes. Cinquez is among those who left the mission. That's when the historical trail goes relatively cold on him. Some accounts have him returning to the mission in 1879, dying there and being buried among the missionaries.[19] Others question whether he died earlier.

The leadership and abilities of Joseph Cinquez are legendary. He united a ship of shackled men from different cultures and languages to overthrow armed slave traders. He learned English quickly enough and well enough to compel Americans to donate to support him and his fellow Africans. He rode the U.S. court system from the lowest court through to the Supreme Court and was successfully defended by a former U.S. president. He accomplished his seemingly impossible goal of returning to Africa, bringing thirty-five men back with him. In the middle of all of this, he visited Lowell and was shown the respect and admiration he had so clearly earned. Whatever he did and wherever he was from the time he returned to Africa to the time he died, I have to believe he thought highly of his time in Lowell and how well he was treated by its people while he was there.

---

1. Ed Brennen, "Bucky Lew Finally Getting His Due," UMass Lowell, February 12, 2024, https://www.uml.edu.
2. Chris Boucher, *The Original Bucky Lew: Basketball's First Black Professional* (Wings ePress, 2023).
3. Black Fives Foundation, "Happy Birthday (1884) to Harry 'Bucky' Lew, America's First Black Pro Hoopster," January 4, 2014, https://www.blackfives.org.
4. University of Massachusetts Lowell Library, "Harry Haskell 'Bucky' Lew (1884–1963)," https://libguides.uml.edu/c.php?g=1125577&p=8215152.
5. Dan O'Brien, "On Thursday, UMass Lowell Will Honor the First Black Professional Basketball Player," Wicked Local, updated February 23, 2024, https://www.wickedlocal.com.
6. African American Registry, "Harry Haskell Lew, Basketball Player Born," https://aaregistry.org.
7. Eva Moseley, "'The Absolute Majority of the Population': Women in Twentieth-Century History Cambridge," https://historycambridge.org.

8. U.S. National Park Service, "Florence Luscomb," https://www.nps.gov.

9. Anna Nowogrodzki, "I Burned with Indignation," MIT Technology Review, October 20, 2020, https://www.technologyreview.com.

10. Ibid.

11. Ibid.

12. Harvard Library, "Papers of Florence Luscomb, 1856–2001," https://hollisarchives.lib.harvard.edu.

13. Maria Karagianis, "Boston's Oldest Protester Still Going Strong at 89," *Boston Globe*, June 27, 1976.

14. Legal Information Institute, "*The United States, Appellants, v. the Libellants and Claimants of the Schooner Amistad, Her Tackle, Apparel, and Furniture, Together With Her Cargo, and the Africans Mentioned and Described in the Several Libels and Claims, Appellees*," https://www.law.cornell.edu.

15. Douglas O. Linder, "Amistad Trials (1839–1840)," Famous Trials, UMKC School of Law, https://famous-trials.com/amistad.

16. Ibid.

17. National Archives, "The Amistad Case," August 15, 2016, https://www.archives.gov.

18. Joseph Sturge, *A Visit to the United States in 1841* (Dexter S. King, 1842), available at the Internet Archive, http://archive.org.

19. Douglas O. Linder, "Amistad Trials (1839–1840)," Famous Trials, UMKC School of Law, https://famous-trials.com/amistad.

CHAPTER 12
HAVERHILL

Vrill, who just started school in Haverhill and is always having to explain that her name rhymes with *frill*, was excited to have a nice kid named Cooper call her over by yelling, "**Hey, Vrill!** Come play!"

FRED AND THERA LUCE

Fred and Thera Luce were an amateur Edwardian archaeology power couple. Despite having five kids, they somehow managed to collect and record over eight thousand ancient artifacts and natural specimens, mostly from Haverhill and surrounding towns. There have always been "collectors." In the early 1900s, one could just walk through a plowed field and find Native American artifacts that had been unearthed. Many people collected in this way, but the Luces took it to the next level. Antoine Trombino-Aponte and Nancy Lebar of the Buttonwoods Museum, which houses the Luce collection, explained that while most collectors at the time just gathered artifacts and tossed them in a cigar box, the Luces "painstakingly recorded them with numbered entries—over 8,000 of them—with descriptive information and sometimes skillful sketches of the artifacts. They recorded ancient site locations, the names of collectors, the dates of discovery, and other information of value to researchers."[1]

The Luces weren't highly educated people. Fred was a farm boy who didn't even graduate high school. It was tilling fields on the farm that got him into archaeology.[2] Thera was apparently the mastermind behind the taxonomy the Luces used to document their findings. Part of the system is based on numbering, but another part involved documenting places based on the geography of Haverhill in the 1910s. While anyone then would have known what their annotations meant, much of it isn't easily understandable to anyone now (think along the lines of "fifty feet west of the Smiths' driveway into the cornfield").[3] Later, Warren Moorehead, a renowned archaeologist who worked extensively with the Peabody Institute in Andover, was brought in to do an official writeup on their sites.[4]

Of course, a modern observer would likely take issue with what the Luces did over one hundred years ago. While the Luces' approach was utterly unremarkable in the 1910s, modern awareness of the injustices suffered by Native Americans and the subsequent plundering of artifacts from their homelands makes us look at the collection a little differently. On one hand, the Luces' careful categorization and preservation of these artifacts offers a

The look on Thera's face says, "I'm doing the same thing he is but in a corset, and he's gonna get all the credit." The Luces in Wellfleet, Massachusetts, 1916. *Courtesy of Buttonwoods Museum.*

picture of Native American life that may otherwise have been destroyed by farming or building. On the other hand, the Luces took what they wanted from potentially sacred sites without any input from the people whose ancestors created those artifacts. There is one particularly interesting case around some items they "collected."

"Collected" is in quotes here because the items I'm referring to are human remains. In 1910, *collected* would have been the word used. These days, we would more likely call it grave robbing. It's difficult now to imagine finding a human bone and picking it up to categorize as you would a piece of pottery. It's extremely upsetting to think of people's remains being treated like "things," bagged and put into basement storage. It's even more upsetting to think of human bones being put on display in museums, which Native American bones sometimes were.[5] This type of treatment is inexcusable, and luckily, many museums and institutions are taking steps to return the human remains in their collections to the proper tribes for reburial. This is the case for human remains formerly in the Luce collection. Ironically, the existence of those bones in the collection and the Luces' careful categorization actually aided in saving a Native burial site in Florida.[6]

After World War I, Fred Luce was unwell. He had nearly died from the flu, and his body was not bouncing back quickly. In the fall of 1919, he took his family to Florida for him to recuperate, and while there, he continued his excavations. One area he excavated was a Native American burial mound he found near the shore of Lake Tibet, outside of Orlando. The Luces collected thousands of artifacts there, among them human remains. As was their habit, they catalogued all the items with an individual number, a map of where they had been found and all their various other notations. The Luces went back to Massachusetts and stowed this collection with the rest in the basement of the Buttonwoods Museum, which in 1995 gave the entire Florida collection to the Peabody Institute of Archaeology at Phillips Andover Academy. It went into another basement, and there it remained.[7]

Fast-forward ninety-three years to 2012. Dr. Ryan Wheeler, a Florida native, had just started a job as the director of the aforementioned Peabody Institute.[8] He realized that much of the Peabody's collection had not been properly catalogued (a.k.a. it had been stuck in a basement and forgotten), so he set about remedying that. Wheeler headed down to the basement to dive in. Because he was from Florida and had to start somewhere, he decided to start with the oddly large number of artifacts from Florida. This was the Luces' collection. In that collection, Wheeler came upon the human remains, with their Luce labels attached.

Here's where things get crazy (in a good way). Ryan Wheeler's job prior to working for the Peabody was official archaeologist for the State of Florida, a job he held for eight years. Part of his role was going to construction sites where archaeologically relevant items had been dug up. Sometimes those construction sites ended up being unmarked grave sites. Wheeler looked at the Luces' documentation, found the map of where the bones had been discovered and realized it wasn't a place he recognized. This was significant because in his years living and working in Florida, he had gotten to know pretty much every archaeological dig going on in the state. He cross-referenced it with a map of known Native American burial sites in Florida and found that, in fact, the Luces' site was not on it.

There can't have been more than a few people in the world who would have been able to look at the Luces' map and immediately see that it was an unrecorded site. Additionally, Dr. Wheeler was (and is) particularly dedicated to the cause of Native American remains' repatriation. So when he realized this omission, he quickly filed the necessary paperwork with Florida to grant the site immediate protection. And good thing he did: as he was making this discovery, a developer in Florida was planning Carmel by the Lake, a luxury home development right on top of where the Luces made their discoveries. The State of Florida put a hold on the development until a proper excavation could be done. They discovered a full burial mound, now called the Macey Mound.[9] The developer set aside a portion of land for the remains of those buried in the mound to be relocated.[10]

Meanwhile, Dr. Wheeler was researching the bones found in his museum. He was able to determine that they were likely Seminole, over ten thousand years old, and that they came from nine different individuals. In 2018, he contacted the Seminole tribe, whom he had worked with many times before, to tell them what he had uncovered. But repatriation is a long process. What follows next is the story of multiple individuals at multiple museums along the East Coast collaborating with the Seminole people during the COVID-19 pandemic to get the bones home. Along the way, more Seminole bones were discovered and repatriated as well. The bones were eventually reburied by the Seminole, with the others from the Macey Mound.[11] They were home.

In 2022, *Flamingo Magazine* ("For Floridians, by Floridians") reported the story and interviewed Tina Osceola, the woman in charge of repatriation of remains for the Seminole tribe. Her response when asked how she felt about the repatriation is telling: "Honestly? I don't think there's any part of it that makes me happy, because it's so incredibly tragic. The only reward we get out of doing this work is stopping it from happening again."[12] Certainly, there is nothing happy about the way these bones were treated. It is incredible, however, how they were brought home.

Nobody in a modern context would say that what the Luces did was okay. The Luces should never have been excavating where they were and should never have taken human remains from where they lay. It is, sadly, the case, however, that in their time, this was considered wholly unproblematic by non-Native people (and nobody was asking the Native Americans their opinion). It is also the case that this story ends as well as it could, with the repatriation of the bones. Meanwhile, the stories of other human remains scattered about museums will likely not end in repatriation due to the lack of records of where they came from. And herein lies the complexity of how to handle people and events like this from our history. Should the Luces have taken the bones? No. Did the fact that they took the bones and catalogued them thoroughly lead to the discovery of the burial mound and the prevention of it being plowed under by a developer? Yes. Is it good that the burial mound was discovered? Yes. Should the Luces be celebrated for it? No. But the complexity of the issue is why it's important to have these conversations—*with* the Native American people, this time.

Willie Johns, former chief justice of the Seminole Tribal Court, gave a eulogy at the reburial. In it, he offered the words he would say to these ancestors given the chance. "I would say, 'Welcome home. Welcome home. And oh, by the way, did you hear? We won. Your people are still here in Florida. And they are doing well.'"[13]

---

1. Buttonwoods Museum, "Introduction to the Luce Collection," https://lucecollection.omeka.net.
2. Buttonwoods Museum, "Trombino-Aponte, Antoine," interview with the author, March 20, 2024.
3. Nancy Morgan Lebar, "Buttonwoods Museum," interview with the author, March 27, 2024.
4. Buttonwoods Museum, "Trombino-Aponte, Antoine," interview with the author, March 20, 2024.
5. Eric Barton, "The Fight to Bring Seminole Ancestors Home," *Flamingo Magazine*, May 23, 2022, https://flamingomag.com.
6. Ibid.

7. Ibid.
8. Warm Mineral Springs Little Salt Spring Archaeological Society, "What the Heck Is the Robert S. Peabody Institute of Archaeology and What Does It Have to [Do] with Florida?," October 10, 2023, https://www.wmslss.org.
9. Eric Barton, "The Fight to Bring Seminole Ancestors Home," *Flamingo Magazine*, May 23, 2022, https://flamingomag.com.
10. Amanda Rabines, "Found Bones of Ancient Indians to Be Reburied," *Orlando Sentinel*, October 4, 2019.
11. Eric Barton, "The Fight to Bring Seminole Ancestors Home," *Flamingo Magazine*, May 23, 2022, https://flamingomag.com.
12. Ibid.
13. Ibid.

CHAPTER 13

QUINCY

Quinn Adams and Quinn Zimmer were in the same class in Quincy, so they went by Quinn A. and **Quinn Z**.

Quincy was one of the towns where the problem wasn't finding enough cool stories, it was taking the zillion cool stories and paring them down to just a few. Quincy is a land of overlaps. Not just one world-changing thing happens there; multiple overlapping world-changing things happen there. Notable people from Quincy aren't just notable in one way; they are notable in multiple ways. Stories about Quincy are easy to start and hard to end, because so many of them naturally flow into one another. I have to believe this is indicative of a well-functioning community organism. Just like how it's hard to separate one bodily process from another (oxygen flows into the lungs, which is pulled out by the blood, which is pumped through the heart, which supplies all the organs…), it's hard to sort Quincy's notable people and moments into neat little boxes. The Summer Seat of Chickataubut's Massachusett people, home of many of the scriveners of the foundations of the United States, birthplace of one of the hallmarks of Massachusetts's cultural identity—Quincy has always been a hotbed of notable occurrences and people.[1]

CHICKATAUBUT

One of the most disheartening things about researching history is the "wall" of primary source availability that one hits when going back prior to the early European invasion of Native American land. The Europeans wrote copiously about what they saw and what they did—all, of course, through the viewpoint of European eyes. For now, I am going to rely on the Massachusett tribe to tell the story of Chickataubut. The following is taken from their website and has its own references, given at the bottom of these pages:

> *In 1631 Gov. Thomas Dudley, Deputy Governor of Massachusetts Bay Colony, speaking of Chickataubut writes; "Upon the River of Neponset, near to the Massachusetts fields dwelled Chickataubut." He also writes, "This man least favors the English of any Sagamore (for so are the Kings with us called as they are Sachems southwards).* We are acquainted with by reason of the old quarrel between him and those of Plymouth wherein he lost seven of his best men."*†
>
> *In a history written by William Hubbard, he tells of "a great rendezvous of all the Massachusetts Indians at the seat of the great Sagamore."*‡
>
> *Beginning with the Charter of the Massachusetts Bay Colony in 1629, "by the grace of King Charles of England" and his claiming of "New England, America and everything in it,"*§ *the Indigenous Massachusett were officially a targeted people. Having already suffered through devastating plagues that had drastically reduced their numbers, and a Massacre at Wessagusset (Weymouth), the order from King Charles was "to reduce or convert to submission the indigenous people of New England."*¶

* Sac'hem, Sagamore, Sagamo are all regional variations of the same title.

† Deputy Governor Thomas Dudley's letter to the Countess of Lincoln (England), Boston, New England, March 12, 1630.

‡ William Hubbard's History 1681.

§ The Charter of Massachusetts Bay 1629; American Colonist's Library- Primary Source Documents, The Avalon Project, Yale Law School.

¶ The Charter of Massachusetts Bay 1629; American Colonist's Library- Primary Source Documents, The Avalon Project, Yale Law School.

Knowing now of this early document mandating the reduction or conversion of the indigenous people of New England, "We must not succumb to the romantic notions that the invading English were peaceful people looking to live in peace and harmony with the Indigenous Massachusett People who had inhabited these lands for thousands of years."[**] *With the sanction of their English King the English invaders were more than ready to "reduce" (kill) the Indigenous people who refused to submit to them.*

Along with the invading pilgrims at Plymouth and later Weymouth, Chickataubut also had to deal with the leaders of the Massachusetts Bay Colony who had settled in the midst of his territory and who were mandated to "reduce or convert to submission"[††] *his people. Chickataubut was not to be converted to submission. He controlled a territory rich in resources, from plentiful whaling/fishing waters and hunting grounds that produced meat and skins, for food clothing and trade, to large and fertile fields of corn, beans, squash and other produce, that along with the fish and meat, fed his people in both summer and winter. The Neponset Quarries produced materials for tool making and weapons for tribal use and for trade. "Chickataubut did not form treaties or agreements that would lead to his ultimate inability to deal effectively with the English from a place of power."*[‡‡]

Clearly, Chickataubut was a powerful leader and shrewd enough to see through the English settlers' attempts to take Massachusett tribal land. He recognized the value of the land he controlled and took seriously his responsibility to his people to keep them fed and housed.

Chickataubut lived with his people at Moswetusett Hummock until 1633 where he was finally struck down by small pox. Knowing the English dictate to "reduce or convert to submission" Chickataubut and his people and knowing Chickataubut to be a great political influence who was unwilling to submit, we the descendants of Chickataubut's Neponset Band believe that the smallpox infection at Passanageset and Moswetusett was intentionally produced by the English through the trade of infected blankets, knowing that the Indigenous people valued them greatly, it would be an efficient way of infecting and thus "reducing" the tribe."[2]

** Gil (Feather on the Moon) Solomon, Lead Sac'hem of the Massachusett Tribe at Ponkapoag.

†† The Charter of Massachusetts Bay 1629; American Colonist's Library- Primary Source Documents, The Avalon Project, Yale Law School.

‡‡ Gil (Feather on the Moon) Solomon, Lead Sac'hem of the Massachusett Tribe at Ponkapoag.

Though the story of Chickataubut ends tragically, his life exemplifies that rare duality: a leader who is both able to show strength internally, in ensuring his people had what they needed to live, and externally, in recognizing the plans of his enemies and protecting his people against them for many years.

JOHN ADAMS, REGULAR GUY

John Adams is synonymous with Quincy, and though I've watched the HBO miniseries on him several times, hence making me a John Adams expert (much like Googling "Why does my head hurt?" makes me a neurologist), I'm always amazed at how much more there is to learn.

One of the best things about John Adams is how strikingly human he comes across as, even after hundreds of years. Some "founding fathers" are spoken of like deities. George Washington is held up on a golden pedestal, and when I think of him, he is always frozen in portrait pose. It's hard to picture Washington just sort of ambling around his kitchen, picking at some grapes, or huffing and rolling his eyes upon realizing he'd misbuttoned his shirt (yes, I know he had people for that). Adams was an incredible thinker—so logical but also so passionate. And also, he was just kind of an eighteenth-century country dude. He jumped back and forth between these roles seamlessly, as indicated by a series of journal entries from 1771. If you don't currently find John Adams relatable, you're about to. All journal/letter excepts are from the Massachusetts Historical Society's online archive.

Here he is on a summer Tuesday, just thinking about manure.

> *Tuesday June 25, 1771*
>
> *At York Court, dined with the judges, and spent the Evening at Ritchies with Bradbury and Hale of Portsmouth, a sensible young Lawyer. Bradbury says there is no need of Dung upon your Mowing Land if you dont feed it in the Fall nor Spring. Let the old Fog remain upon it, and die and rot and be washed into the Ground, and dont suffer your Cattle to tread upon it and so poach and break the soil, and you will never want any Dung.*
>
> *Recipe to make Manure.*
>
> *Take the Soil and Mud, which you cutt up and throw out when you dig Ditches in a Salt Marsh, and put 20 Load of it in a heap. Then take 20 Loads of common Soil or mould of Upland and Add to the other. Then to*

> *the whole add 20 Loads of Dung, and lay the whole in a Heap, and let it lay 3 months, then take your Spades And begin at one End of the Heap, and dig it up and throw it into another Heap, there let it lie, till the Winter when the Ground is frozen, and then cart it on, to your English Grass Land.—Ten or 20 Loads to an Acre, as you choose.—Rob. Temple learnt it in England, and first practised it at Ten Hills. From him the Gentry at Cambridge have learnt it, and they all Practise it.*
>
> *I will bring up 20 or 30 Loads, of this Salt Marsh Mud, and lay it in my Cow Yard upon the Sea Weed that is there, bring up that which lies in the Road by James Bracketts as we go to Mr. Quincys.... Would not a Load of fresh meadow Mud, and a Load of Salt Meadow Mud with some Sand, and some dung &c. make a good Mixture.*[3]

This is pretty funny in its own right. But it gets better. So on Tuesday, he's waxing poetic in his journal about mixing up mud, dung and marsh. Then on Wednesday, he writes *about yesterday* (a.k.a. "Dung Tuesday") the following:

> *Wednesday June 26, 1771*
>
> *Yesterday I had a good deal of Conversation with Judge Trowbridge. He seems alarmed about the Powers of the Court of Probate. He says if Judge Danforth was to die Tomorrow, and the Governor was to offer that Place to him, he would not take it, because he thinks it ought always to be given to some Judge of the Inferiour Court, and then, some one Lawyer might be found in each County who would take a Seat upon the Inferiour Bench, if he could be made a Judge of Probate at the same Time. He says he is utterly against Foster Hutchinsons holding the Probate Office in Boston, if he takes his Place upon the Superior Bench—and if the Governor is an integral Part, of the Court of Probate, the Supreme ordinary, i.e. if he is not, with the Members of the Council, only Primus inter Pares but has a Negative upon all their Decrees as Governor Shirley, Govr. Bernard and the late Secretary, were of Opinion, he thinks we may be in great Danger from the Court of Probate, and Judge Russell always opposed every Attempt to extend the Power of the Court of Probate.—He used to say We might have Bishops here, and the Court of Probate might get into their Hands, and therefore We ought to be upon our Guard.*[4]

So apparently on Tuesday he has this big conversation about the structure of the probate court and a potential threat to the judicial system, but that's not what he writes about. He writes about manure. It's not until the *next* day he's like, "Oh yeah and by the way, I forgot to mention this thing about the courts…"

I love this guy.

This passage is also particularly relatable. He's traveling with a group of people from north to south along the Massachusetts coast, and he's just straight-up grouchy:

> *Tuesday July 2, 1771*
>
> *This has been the most flat, insipid, spiritless, tasteless journey that ever I took, especially from Ipswich. I have neither had Business nor Amusement, nor Conversation. It has been a moaping, melancholly Journey upon the whole. I slumber, and moap, away the Day.*[5]

We've all been there, man.

As cool as John Adams is, his wife, Abigail, may be even cooler. We all know she entreated him to "remember the ladies" in drafting the laws of the new country (*cough cough* John—the vote?), and John Adams's journals show how much he respected her insights and opinions.

The Massachusetts Historical Society has all John Adams's journals online for anyone to look at, but even more fun (in my opinion) are the letters between John and Abigail, back to before they were married. I don't really speak fluent Eighteenth Century, but I think those early letters might be a little sassy! Work with me here…

Abigail writes to John, whom she has nicknamed "Lysander":

> *April 12, 1764*
>
> *Here am I all alone, in my Chamber, a mere Nun I assure you, after professing myself thus will it not be out of Character to confess that my thoughts are often employ'd about Lysander, "out of the abundance of the Heart, the mouth speaketh," and why Not the Mind thinketh.*

(My interpretation: "Hey boo… I'm here all by myself in my bedroom just thinkin' about you…")

> *Me thinks I have abundance to say to you. What is next? O that I should have been extreemly* [sic] *glad to have seen you to Day. Last Fast Day, if you remember, we spent together, and why might we not this? Why I can tell you, we might, if we had been together, have been led into temptation. I dont mean to commit any Evil, unless setting up late, and thereby injuring our Health, may be called so.*

(My interpretation: "I wish we'd gotten to see each other today, though I could see things getting a little spicy if we had. Sooo, probably good that we didn't.")

> *PS Let me hear from you soon as possible, and as often. By sending your Letters to the Doctor believe you may get conveyance often. I rejoice to hear you feel so comfortable. Still be careful, good folks are scarce. My Mamma has just been up, and asks to whom I am writing. I answerd not very readily. Upon my hesitating—Send my Love say'd she to Mr. Adams, tell him he has my good wishes for his Safty.*[6]

(My interpretation: "Hit me back, cutie. Sending notes through your boy the Doctor might be safe, but be careful—we'll get in big trouble if these love notes get intercepted… Eek! My mom totally just called me out on writing to you. But I think she likes you…)

It's a great disservice to modern people when highly accomplished people from the past are put on pedestals, characterized as infallible, their quirks and failures overlooked. Recognizing these historical figures as human, just like us, makes them so much more accessible and makes history so much more relevant. We have all thought about other stuff during important meetings, the way John Adams was likely thinking about manure at some point during his judges' meeting. We have all been plain old grumpy and mopey and "blecch" for periods of time as John Adams was on his journey. We have all sent a flirty text or note like John and Abigail did when they were courting. And maybe, just maybe, that means that like John and Abigail Adams, we can all do something great.

THE LEGENDARY DUNKIN' DONUTS

You didn't think you were going to get through a book on Massachusetts without a reference to Dunkin', did you? You certainly weren't going to get through a book that includes Quincy history, as Quincy is the glorious seat of the founding of the Massachusetts baked good and beverage icon. Let's just get one thing out of the way. I don't even care if you like coffee. Or donuts. Or if you're "more of a Starbucks type." Whatever the case, you simply have to acknowledge the cultural significance Dunkin' holds in modern Massachusetts.

Three young Massachusetts natives rejoice at the sight of a Dunk's sign. *Author's collection.*

To start, let's clear up the vernacular. Dunkin' Donuts is the long-term name of the establishment. They changed it to Dunkin' in 2018 to reflect their changing menu. While the donuts weren't going anywhere, Dunkin's coffee had become the star of the show, and their food offerings had evolved way past just donuts. So now it may be officially called Dunkin', but I'm not sure I've ever heard anyone say, "Hey, I'm going by Dunkin', want me to pick you up anything?" They'd say Dunks. It's always Dunks.

William Rosenberg started Dunks in Quincy in 1948, as Open Kettle, but we don't talk about that. In 1950, he changed the name to Dunkin' Donuts (whew) and started expanding almost immediately.[7] His friends and family were probably not surprised. Rosenberg was a natural entrepreneur. Take this story from his 2002 obituary:

> *Mr. Rosenberg demonstrated an entrepreneurial spirit at a young age. As a teenager during the Great Depression, he once carted a block of ice to a racetrack on a hot summer day and sold ice chips at 10 cents a piece, bringing home $171.*[8]

One dollar during the Great Depression is about eighteen dollars now.[9] That means he grossed $3,078 that day. That's what a lot of people made in a year. I couldn't find the price of an ice block then, but I'm confident that regardless, Rosenberg walked away with a solid chunk of change. This episode demonstrates that Rosenberg knew how to make money, and he was about to do it up big-time.

Dunks wasn't Rosenberg's first business venture (or wasn't his second, if you count the ice block). In 1945, he converted an old telephone company truck, giving it an insulated space, a flip-up side and fold-out shelves. From this truck, he sold coffee, pastries and sandwiches at factories and construction sites. Yes, the guy who started Dunks also invented the canteen truck. Mind: blown. Within four years, Rosenberg's company, Industrial Luncheon Service, had two hundred canteen trucks, ran twenty-five cafeterias and also had a vending division. Rosenberg noted that 40 percent of the company's revenue was coming from coffee and donuts, which compelled him to open a stand-alone coffee and donut joint.[10] That joint became Dunks.

This part of the narrative kind of mars my vision of the Dawn of Dunks. I've always had it in my head that this scrappy guy took a chance on himself, saved up and opened this donut shop on a wing and a prayer. In fact, that whole "wing and a prayer" part happened back when he started Industrial Luncheon Service. By the time he opened ~~Open Kettle~~ Dunks, he was already a very successful businessperson. I'll get over it.

By 1954, he had five Dunks, and world domination was underway.[11] In 1955, Rosenberg began franchising, and by 1965, there were over one hundred locations in the United States. Franchising is what allowed Dunks to really explode. Business-minded individuals saw the chance to get in on a company that was doing well, without the risk and headache of having to start a brand-new business from scratch. While the concept of franchising existed prior to Rosenberg, he really developed the concept into what we think of as franchising today. He founded the International Franchise Association, and many of his innovations and ideas remain integral to the franchising world.[12]

A non-historical aside about franchising: most of Greater Boston has, at some point, fantasized about how rich they'd be if they owned a Dunks. It's tough to look at the lines of people each shelling out five bucks for an iced coffee (even when it's three degrees out) and not dream about what you'd do with that money. Sadly, franchise owners don't get to just take all that money and throw it in a giant Scrooge McDuck money bin to swim around in. Let me break down the Dunks franchising situation for you.

First, you need to have $250,000 liquid and be able to show at least $500,000 net worth. For that, you get about two weeks of training plus access to online training, access to downloadable Dunks marketing materials and access to Dunks real estate experts. You are required to purchase Dunks' mobile app system and order/supply management systems, so that's extra. In short, you have to have a solid chunk of change at your disposal to get in on a Dunks location. Oh, and don't think you're going to just sit behind a desk somewhere. Franchise owners are expected to work a full shift just about every day for the first year.[13] For this, your store may bring in around $1 million a year in sales, but after all your expenses, you can expect to take home about $100,000. Because of this ratio, most Dunks are owned by franchising conglomerates that own many locations.[14] Sorry to crush your dreams.

So before that little dive into franchising, we were back in 1965, with about one hundred Dunks locations, most of which were franchised. At this point, William Rosenberg's son Bob had taken the reins. They went public in 1968 as part of the Universal Food Systems chain and were bought by Allied Lyons, which also owns Baskin-Robbins. Yes, that's how Baskin-Robbins got involved in all this.

From 1968 to now, the story of Dunks is just growth, growth, growth. Acquisitions, subsidiaries, yadda yadda business things and boom: in 2023, the company had $1.4 billion in sales across over nine thousand U.S. stores and four thousand international stores spread across forty-five countries.[15] But as big and as worldly as Dunks gets, it'll always be the coffee and donut shop that started right on the circle down in Quincy.

CAPTAIN HANSEN GREGORY, DONUT INVENTOR

Strangely enough, none of this could have happened without the invention of another Quincy resident, Captain Hansen Gregory. Back around 1858, Gregory was a sixteen-year-old cabin-boy-turned-sea-cook aboard all kinds of vessels sailing out of Camden, Maine. Doughnuts kind of existed then. They were called "twisters," "fried cakes" or, tellingly, "sinkers." They were commonly pieces of dough cut into diamond shapes and fried. The name "sinkers" came along because they were shaped and cooked in a way that caused them to fry on the edges but be raw-ish in the center and also soak up a lot of grease from the fryer. They were purportedly so heavy they'd sink in your stomach and give you all kinds of digestion issues. Gross.

As cook, Gregory heard a lot of complaints about his "sinkers." He was sick of it, so took to the kitchen to try to fix the problem. A *New York Times* article at the time of his nomination to the Baking Hall of Fame by the National Donut Committee (yes, these are both real things) detailed the changes he made. First, he added more shortening and leavening agent (baking powder or yeast) to "puff" the donuts up more. He waited until the frying fat was superhot, such that the dough wouldn't absorb as much of it when cooking. These things helped, but Gregory wasn't satisfied. He realized that the shape itself was aiding in the hockey puck–like nature of the dessert. Because it was one solid lump of dough, there was no way for the middle to puff up, simply due to the weight of it and its distance and insulation from the heat of the frying fat. So he cut a hole in the middle. Bingo. The hole allowed the fat to cook the tube of dough from multiple angles and gave the dough the space to puff up all around. The sailors loved them, and their nickname went from "sinkers" to "life preservers."[16]

Recounting the story to his buddies at a doughnut shop in next-door Southie, Gregory said (please read in classic seafarer/pirate voice), "I took the cover off the ship's tin pepper box, and—I cut into the middle of that donut the first hole ever seen by mortal eyes!"[17]

Gregory had a tinsmith make him a cutter with two concentric circles: one to cut the doughnut from the sheet of dough and the other to simultaneously cut the hole out of the center. He gave one to his mom, who made doughnuts and sold them to a great reception. The style spread, and as soon as 1877, a recipe book featured a recipe for doughnuts, which called for cutting them into rings.

Gregory lived at the Sailor's Snug Harbor, a home founded in 1852 by Captain Josiah Bacon for sailors "broken down by infirmities brought on by diseases in foreign clinics, expenses, and hardships."[18] He lived until age eighty-nine and died and is buried in Quincy at the Snug Harbor Sailors Cemetery.

I can't help but wonder what Gregory would have thought had he known a billion-dollar business would start out of his very town, based on the confection he invented. It is indeed a small world.

---

1. The Massachusett Tribe at Ponkapoag "Chickataubut," https://massachusetttribe.org.
2. Ibid.
3. John Adams, "Diary 20," June 20, 1774, Adams Family Papers at Massachusetts Historical Society, https://www.masshist.org.

4. Ibid.
5. Ibid.
6. Abigail Smith, letter to John Adams, April 12–13, 1764 [electronic edition], Adams Family Papers: An Electronic Archive, Massachusetts Historical Society.
7. Dunkin', "Dunkin' Donuts History," https://news.dunkindonuts.com.
8. *New York Times*, "William Rosenberg, 86, Founder of Dunkin' Donuts," September 23, 2002.
9. Statista, "Value of the US Dollar 1635–2020," https://www.statista.com.
10. Dunkin', "Dunkin' Donuts Founder Passes Away," September 22, 2002, https://news.dunkindonuts.com.
11. Dunkin', "A Dozen Things You Didn't Know About Dunkin'," July 19, 2018, https://news.dunkindonuts.com/blog.
12. Dunkin', "Dunkin' Donuts Founder Passes Away," September 22, 2002, https://news.dunkindonuts.com.
13. Dunkin', "How Can I Become a Franchise Owner with Dunkin," https://www.dunkinfranchising.com.
14. Franchise Business Review, "Dunkin' Franchise Review 2022: Costs, Profits and Comparisons," March 20, 2022, https://franchisebusinessreview.com.
15. Zippia, "Dunkin' Donuts Revenue: Annual, Quarterly, and Historic," December 14, 2021, https://www.zippia.com.
16. Find a Grave, "Capt Hanson Crockett Gregory (1831–1921)," https://www.findagrave.com.
17. New England Historical Society, "The Maine Ship Captain Who Invented the Modern Donut," May 22, 2014, https://newenglandhistoricalsociety.com.
18. Leslie Landrigan, "The Clipper Ship That Built the Sailors Snug Harbor," New England Historical Society, October 9, 2014, https://newenglandhistoricalsociety.com.

CHAPTER 14

LEICESTER

"**Lester**, why do you have to spell your name so weird?" asked Hannah.
"What do you mean?" replied Leicester.

THE UN-HAUNTED SPIDER GATES CEMETERY (WOMP WOMP)

"The eighth gate to Hell is supposed to be located somewhere in Friends Cemetery in Leicester, Massachusetts, a rural town just outside Worcester."[1] …I'm listening. "At midnight, walk around the gravestone of Marmaduke Earle (b. 1749–d. 1839) and then rest your head on it. You will hear him speak to you."[2] …Tell me more.

These stories come from Quaker Friends Cemetery in Leicester, better known as Spider Gates Cemetery due to the very cool spidery-looking iron gates around it. If you look for any Leicester history, Spider Gates is probably the first thing you'll find, so I felt it needed to go in this book. Plus, I was pretty psyched about a haunted cemetery. I scoured the Internet for any firsthand experiences with any spookiness. They were few and far between.

I did find a ton of rumors though, in addition to the two I already mentioned. Some are quite creative:

1. There are rocks with runes carved on them in front of the gates.
2. The ground oozes white slime.
3. There's a second (or third?) cemetery nearby that you can find only once.
4. If you drink from a nearby pond, something evil will follow you home, and you'll need the help of a witch to remove it.
5. If you enter the cemetery with bad intentions, an eight-foot-tall gatekeeper will lock you inside.
6. There is an oak tree with a rope hanging from it known as the Hanging Tree. Someone committed suicide there, and their ghost still haunts the cemetery.
7. A demonic creature has been heard roaring in the woods.
8. Satanists have permission to conduct their rituals in part of the cemetery called the Altar.[3]

The cemetery is located in the woods and, apparently, quite hard to find, which I'm sure adds to its spookiness. You know what else is apparently quite hard to find? Any definitive information on Spider Gates Cemetery. There are a million rumors, but pretty much nobody who has actually written about having a spooky experience there. And I went to Reddit, where you can generally find someone claiming to have had any experience you could imagine. Even the rumors are self-contradictory. There is a second cemetery that can be found only once. No, it's a third cemetery. *This* is the "hanging tree." No, *that* is the "hanging tree." It used to have big, tall gates that said, "Quaker Cemetery." No, these are the original gates. On and on and on…

I really wanted to be creeped out by Spider Gates Cemetery, which is a low bar: I'm notoriously easy to creep out. But alas, it just seems like a really pretty, old cemetery in the woods. Sorry, everyone.

SAMUEL MAY

Samuel May was pastor of the Leicester Unitarian Church from 1835 to 1846. He was a prominent abolitionist whose Leicester house was a stop on the Underground Railroad. May was one of the original founders of the Leicester Anti-Slavery Society and a prominent voice urging other ministers to take a stronger position on slavery.[4]

When it came to causes he believed in, May was not afraid to take personal risks. He was instrumental in the 1851 rescue of a Black man from Syracuse, New York, named William Jerry McHenry, who went by Jerry. Jerry, who had escaped enslavement, was arrested at his workplace, where he made barrels. He was told he was being arrested for theft, but after he had been cuffed, the marshals told him he was in fact being arrested under the Fugitive Slave Act, a law that allowed for the arrest of any Black person even suspected of being a runaway slave. Jerry fought to escape his arresters but was unable to. Luckily, an antislavery convention (with May in attendance) was happening in the city at the time. Also luckily, the wife of a local judge had heard of the plans and informed local abolitionists to be ready, and thanks to May's planning, they were. Upon Jerry's arrest, the convention attendees rang the church bells, and a crowd of abolitionists went to the court where Jerry was being arraigned. They tried to free him on the spot, and though he escaped momentarily, he was quickly recaptured. After the ruckus, the judge postponed the arraignment until later in the day. Word continued to spread, and more abolitionists gathered, intent on freeing Jerry. When the arraignment started, the protesters physically broke down the courtroom door with a battering ram. (That's impressive.) The court deputies recognized they had no chance of keeping Jerry captive and turned him over to the crowd, who hid him and eventually transported him to safety in Canada.[5]

Two weeks after the rescue, May delivered a speech to another New York abolitionist convention and said this about the event:

> *But when the people saw a man dragged through the streets, chained and held down in a cart by four or six others who were upon him; treated as if he were the worst of felons; and learnt that it was only because he had assumed to be what God made him to be, a man, and not a slave—when this came to be known throughout the streets, there was a mighty throbbing of the public heart; an all but unanimous up rising against the outrage.*

> *There was no concert of action except that to which a common humanity impelled the people. Indignation flashed from every eye. Abhorrence of the Fugitive Slave Bill poured in burning words from every tongue. The very stones cried out.*[6]

At the time of the rescue, May was pastor of a church in Syracuse, having left Leicester some five years prior. He did not leave of his own volition. May was considered quite radical at the time for his strong abolitionist views, in addition to his belief in women's rights, Native American rights and pacifism. He had been stirring up controversy in Leicester with sermons like "The Rights and Condition of Women," delivered in 1846. Additionally, he did not believe in segregation within the pews of the church, which ruffled the feathers of some of the less forward-thinking parishioners. As it happens, many of those less forward-thinking parishioners were the mill owners who held all the money and power in town.[7] May was asked to leave the parish, with those parishioners claiming he spent too much time on his abolitionist work and not enough leading the congregation.[8]

May ended up living in Syracuse for the rest of his life, though the house where he lived in Leicester retains the moniker the May House. It was owned for many years by Becker College, a small liberal arts school that closed in 2021. Efforts are currently underway to convert the May House into an educational and community center.[9] A center that offers educational opportunities and that brings together a diverse community of individuals from around Leicester would be a fitting tribute to the man for whom the house is named.

---

1. Peter Muise, "Spider Gates Cemetery: Portals to Hell and College Kids in Robes," *New England Folklore* (blog), September 6, 2016, https://newenglandfolklore.blogspot.com.
2. Ibid.
3. Ibid.; Wicked Crime, "Episode 12: The Legend of Spider Gates Cemetery," October 11, 2020, https://wickedxcrime.wordpress.com.
4. Don Milmore, "Samuel Joseph May," National Abolition Hall of Fame and Museum, 2017, https://www.nationalabolitionhalloffameandmuseum.org.

5. Timothy McDonnell, "The *Jerry Rescue* in Syracuse, NY," Geography of York State!, http://www.nygeo.org.
6. Daniel Connors, "Today in History: The Jerry Rescue," Onondaga Historical Association, October 1, 2014, https://www.cnyhistory.org.
7. Women Transcending Boundaries, "Learning about Abolitionist Samuel Joseph May," February 12, 2023, https://wtb.org.
8. Worcester Women's History Project, "Samuel May, Jr. (1810–1899)," https://www.wwhp.org.
9. Brian Lee, "Symbol of Underground Railroad," *Worcester Telegram & Gazette*, last updated February 19, 2021, https://www.telegram.com.

CHAPTER 15

DORCHESTER

When their doorbell of their three-family rang in Dorchester, Abby yelled to her husband, "**Door, Chester**!"

Warning: heads up to all women who were tweens in the late '80s/early '90s. This next chapter may be upsetting, not for its content per se but rather for its inclusion in a history book. I'm so sorry to do this to you, but it's about New Kids on the Block. There is no clear consensus on how far back something has to be to qualify as "history," but Joey, Jon, Jordan, Danny and Donnie started their rise to infinite power in 1985, and forty years falls within the range of most opinions on "far back enough to be called 'history.'" If you need to take a moment, please do. I'll wait.

NKOTB and the Franklin Park Zoo bear pens are the two stories I investigated for the Dorchester chapter. They seemed unconnected, aside from Danny Wood getting a little furrily ursine there for a while. Then I learned that NKOTB's second performance was at—Franklin Park! Shame on me for thinking that any two things from Dorchester don't share some sort of connection. Plus, as it turns out, both NKOTB and the bear pens are having a moment. In 2024, New Kids released an album and went on tour for the first time in ten years, and the bear pens secured $800,000 in funding toward fixing them up from their unseemly state. So it looks like 2024 was a year of new beginnings for both of these Dorchester icons.

NKOTB, OBV

New Kids on the Block (NKOTB for those of us in the know) is famously Boston. Accents and all, the boys proudly wore their Dorchester "street" roots as a badge of honor (except for Joey McIntyre, who was from the 'burbs). They were brought together by producer Maurice Starr, who sent talent agent Mary Alford to the streets of Boston to look for tough guys who could sing, rap and dance. Donnie Wahlberg, fourteen, auditioned for Alford and became the first member to be brought on. From there, the band grew through Wahlberg. He pulled in his thirteen-year-old brother Mark and his friend Jamie Kelly. The trio recruited Jordan and Jonathan Knight, another Dorchester sibling set. Another Wahlberg buddy, Danny Wood, wowed Starr with his breakdancing skills and joined the team.[1] Early on, Mark Wahlberg left the group, and Jamie Kelly was dismissed for lack of commitment. Maurice Starr needed someone for high notes, and since castratos haven't been a thing for a few hundred years, he pulled in Joey McIntyre, a twelve-year-old from Needham. Talk about culture shock: a twelve-year-old kid from a swanky suburb gets thrown in with a bunch of older street toughs. Bravo to McIntyre for getting through that transition.

The initial two Wahlberg brothers did not make up a significant percentage of the Wahlberg children. There were nine of them. Nine. They lived in a typical triple-decker in Dorchester well before gentrification crept in. The Wahlbergs' mother (*of nine*) spoke to DotNews about the environment in the neighborhood when she was raising her *nine* children: "They tried to evict a family and we wouldn't let them in to evict them....We all stood in front of her apartment—hysterical!—but that's the way it was then. We all looked out for each other."[2]

The Knights grew up in a nearby Victorian mansion, but it wasn't a typical "mansion life" for them. Their father was an Episcopal priest and operated the twenty-three-room, nine-bedroom Victorian as a sort of foster home for troubled kids.[3] The carriage house behind the main house was the backdrop for several NKOTB promotional photo shoots and a music video. Danny Wood also grew up in Dorchester and lived there through many of the NKOTB years. His dad lived in the same house until 2006. Danny lost his mom in 1999 (years after the band broke up) to breast cancer and started a foundation in her honor.[4]

While none of the New Kids live in Dorchester anymore, a location of the Wahlbergs' restaurant Wahlburgers opened there in 2018. It's run by Paul, one of the other *nine* Wahlberg children. The menu features nods to Dorchester, including the O.F.D. ("originally from Dorchester") burger and the Double-Decker (almost a triple-decker). The Wahlbergs also have a fine dining restaurant in Hingham called Alma Nove after their mom, Alma, and her *nine* children (*nove* means "nine" in Italian. As in *nine* children).

The members of NKOTB have done an impressive job of staying out of really embarrassing or heartbreaking situations since the band broke up in 1995.[5] That's saying a lot, given the way a lot of '90s pop stars have ended up. Fingers crossed that they stay on the straight and narrow, because unlike with the bear pens, I don't think the City of Boston is going to pledge $800,000 toward their rehabilitation.

The Franklin Park Zoo Bear Pens

"But there are no bears at the Franklin Park Zoo," you might say, and you'd be correct. But back in 1912, when the zoo opened, there were quite a few. And they were housed in the still-existent Franklin Park Zoo Bear Pens.[6] The pens are essentially ruins now. You can go see them in the area near the zoo called Long Crouch Woods, but be careful. What's left is a tangled mess of iron spikes and rubble bearing minimal resemblance to the grand spectacle the pens once were.

Franklin Park is the terminus of the Emerald Necklace, a seven-mile string of parks that runs through Boston. The parks were designed by Frederick Olmsted, who is famous for his work around the country, including the U.S. Capitol in Washington, D.C.; New York's Central Park; and Boston's Arnold Arboretum. Franklin Park itself is its own entity, though many people now know it only as it relates to the zoo. But the 527-acre park was considered the "crown jewel" of Olmsted's Emerald Necklace project. It encompasses land not only in Dorchester but in Jamaica Plain and Roxbury as well.

A zoo had always been part of the plan for Franklin Park, though Olmsted himself was not a big fan of zoos.[7] In 1910, the mayor of Boston, John Fitzgerald, initiated the zoo project with the hopes that it would bring more people to Franklin Park. He chose Franklin Park as the site for the zoo based on its easy access to the trolley system and its sprawling acreage. Olmsted had passed away in 1903, so Fitzgerald hired Arthur Shurcliff, who had worked with Olmsted on Franklin Park, to design the zoo. He did not disappoint.

Two of Shurcliff's buildings are still in use at the zoo—interestingly, the first two buildings that were completed and opened to the public. The William Austin Bird House, now known as Bird's World, was the first structure to be completed. The Aquatic Flying Cage, now called Raptor Ridge, was the second. While these buildings opened in early 1912 to great acclaim, the opening of the bear pens later that same year was the "big show."

An article in the *Boston Globe* reported that over ten thousand people came to the zoo on October 3, 1912, to see the bears released into the new pens. Titled "Antics of Bears at Zoo Keep Crowd Roaring," the article describes the release of the twelve bears in front of the giant crowd. "The two young [Russian brown] bears ran around the pen, jumped on the big tree trunk and on the rocks, knocked each other over, climbed the trees and cut up such capers that the people yelled their approval."[8] The crowds felt safe due to the "twelve foot iron fence" surrounding the pen, "topped with a hood with spikes," making it "insurmountable."[9] (Aside: you'd think with the "unsinkable" *Titanic* having sunk just six months before, the reporter would have been wary of using such absolutist words as "insurmountable.") The day brought in $10,000 to the zoo (in today's dollars, that's about $323,000), which is particularly impressive given there was no entrance fee at the time.

The Franklin Park Zoo bear cages, bears not included. *Courtesy of Library of Congress Historic American Buildings Survey.*

For 1912, the bear pens achieved the height of animal welfare standards. "The three pens occupy more than an acre. The open quarters are concerted and underneath the concrete is an air space, so that there is no danger of the animals getting rheumatism, and the under floor is strewn with broken glass so rats can't find lodgment there. The housing quarters in the rear are spacious and fitted up with great care."[10] The pens were deemed finer than those in Paris or London and gave credence to Fitzgerald's claim that the zoo was the finest in the world.

The bears continued to be a major attraction, and the bear pens continued to be lauded. A November 1919 *Boston Globe* article describes the zoo animals' first "Thanksgiving Dinner" (presumably, the idea was put off for the years encompassing World War I). "Suddenly underkeepers carrying baskets of raw mutton appeared. Instantly the bears set up a weird calling, half growl and half wail. They snarled at each other and reached through the bars. Dexterously the keepers ripped the chunks of meat into the cage and the bears tumbled over each other to reach them."[11] (Honestly, raw mutton and cages aside, that doesn't sound too different from Thanksgiving in my family.) This same article spent an odd amount of time praising the cleanliness of the bear pens: "No dining room could be cleaner than those cages. The great open spaces—the cages are among the largest bear cages in the country—were amazingly clean. When the reporter went to the back of the dens…the floor and walls looked as if they have just been scrubbed—as indeed they had."[12] It goes on. The bears and their domicile were clearly a source of pride for the city.

In 1920, two million people visited the zoo, which is particularly impressive considering that the population of Boston at the time was only 750,000. As was the case with many leisure-centric attractions, attendance took a dip during the years of the Great Depression, though because admission remained free, the zoo was still a popular attraction. However, funding for the zoo declined in the face of the massive social needs of Boston residents during that time. World War II presented a similar problem. With humans' food being rationed, the copious amount of meat and other food it took to keep the bears and other animals alive became a sore subject.

> *In January 1945, the New York Times reported that city councilor William Keenan, proposed a plan to shoot the animals at the Franklin Park Zoo and to use their remains as fertilizer.*[13]

Yikes.

By the 1950s, the rationing and war funding issues had been resolved, but many other factors were working against the bears. Many people had moved to the suburbs and drove cars now, and since the park and the zoo hadn't been planned with parking, they became a hassle to visit. Many other attractions and zoos were popping up, crowding the field and competing for potential visitors' attention. And because the zoo was entirely open, with no gates or fences, safety was becoming an issue.[14] The safety issue affected the bear pens in particular, since they were relatively far away from the rest of the zoo attractions. With all these factors working against the bears, the pens were closed in 1954.[15]

The bear pens (and the nearby raccoon enclosure) weren't demolished once they were closed. The zoo administration essentially just built a big fence around the zoo—and left those structures on the outside. The pens fell into serious disrepair but never left the collective conscious of the city. That area of the park has walking trails running through it, so the pens never really fell off the map. Thankfully, though most of the structures are gone, the beautiful carved relief has stayed in decent condition. It depicts two bears on either side of a shield featuring Boston's skyline as it looked in 1912.

Recent interest in the bear pens has spurred an effort to rehabilitate them into something new—or at least maintain what's left of them. The city recently pledged to invest $800,000 toward ADA compliance updates and safety measures, as a first step toward potentially turning them into something more. Members of the surrounding community, mostly Dorchester residents, have suggested turning the "pools" into splash pads and adding other kids' play structures or creating an amphitheater and event space.[16] For lovers of architecture, nature and bears (I am all three), the idea of this space becoming active again is exciting. The pens are too beautiful and too storied to let slip away.

---

1. Sarah Kettler, "The Hurdles New Kids on the Block Overcame Before Enjoying Pop Music Success," Biography, May 17, 2024, https://www.biography.com.
2. Simon Rios, "The Wahlbergs and Dorchester: A Complicated Story," *Dorchester Reporter*, May 31, 2018, https://www.dotnews.com.
3. Mark Washburn, "Dorchester Mansion Is Former New Kids on the Block Home," Coastal Neighborhoods, October 23, 2021, https://www.coastalneighborhoods.com.
4. Julie Loffredi, "5 New Kids on the Block Landmarks Fans Must See," Fox News, July 6, 2015, https://www.foxnews.com.

5. New Kids on the Block, https://www.nkotb.com.
6. Chloe Courtney Bohl, "What's the Story Behind the Abandoned Bear Cages in Franklin Park?" Boston.com, September 20, 2023, https://www.boston.com.
7. Julie Arrison, "Historic American Buildings Survey—The Old Bear Dens," Olmstedbooks, March 30, 2008. https://olmstedbooks.blogspot.com.
8. *Boston Globe*, "Antics of Bears at Zoo Keep Crowds Roaring," October 4, 1912.
9. Ibid.
10. Ibid.
11. Ibid.
12. Ibid.
13. Julie Arrison, "Historic American Buildings Survey—The Old Bear Dens," Olmstedbooks, March 30, 2008. https://olmstedbooks.blogspot.com.
14. U.S. National Park Service "Bear Dens," https://www.nps.gov.
15. Ibid.
16. Chloe Courtney Bohl, "What's the Story Behind the Abandoned Bear Cages in Franklin Park?" Boston.com, September 20, 2023, https://www.boston.com.

CHAPTER 16

BILLERICA

Chris said to his buddies as they pulled over, "**Bill, Rick, uh**, maybe it's not a good idea to pick up hitchhikers in front of the Billerica Prison."

One of the most fun towns to watch non–Massachusetts natives try to pronounce is Billerica. Clearly, they think, it must be *Bill-Erica*, like the two names put together. Alas, no. It is not. To make things even more interesting, beyond that initial pronunciation faux pas lies another layer of complexity that exemplifies much of what makes language so fascinating.

If Billerica is mentioned on the news or by anyone *not* from Billerica, it's pronounced *Bill-RICK-uh*. Pronouncing it this way, however, is a clear indicator to anyone who *is* from Billerica that you are an outsider. Native Billericans almost all say *BRICK-uh*.

Billerica was named after Billericay in England, where many of the early settlers were from. (Why did they drop the *y* at the end? No clue.) In England, Billericay is (currently) pronounced *BILL-uh-RICK-ee*, which is much closer to the way it looks. Presumably, the Massachusetts settlers originally pronounced it *BILL-uh-RICK-uh*, if in fact they were trying to be true to the town's namesake. So at some point, *BILL-uh-RICK-uh* seems to have morphed into *Bill-RICK-uh* in the way that all language constantly evolves. The big question is: Will the native Billericans' next-level evolution, *BRICK-uh*, eventually creep out beyond town lines and unseat the current popular pronunciation? Or will the current popular pronunciation eventually overpower the native Billericans' *BRICK-uh*? Only time will tell.

YANKEE DOODLE

Every American kid learns the old-timey, goofily patriotic ditty "Yankee Doodle," and every American parent dreads having to explain 1,500 times what feathers and hats have to do with macaroni. The song started out as a way well-groomed British soldiers, in their fancy-dancy finely tailored red uniforms, would mock the ragtag colonial soldiers in their unrefined battle duds.

Most of us know the first verse and the chorus, and for most of us, this is more than enough "Yankee Doodle."

Yankee Doodle went to town
A-riding on a pony,
Stuck a feather in his cap
And called it macaroni.

Yankee Doodle keep it up,
Yankee Doodle dandy,
Mind the music and the step,
And with the girls be handy.

What none of us need to know are the following fifteen-plus verses. That's right, there are at least fifteen more verses of Yankee Doodle.

Another thing none of us need to know is what it's like to be tarred and feathered. What's the connection? Oddly, the tarring and feathering of a Billerica man in colonial Boston is the reason "Yankee Doodle" is such a prominent part of American culture.[1]

It was March 7, 1775, two years after the Boston Tea Party and just over a month before the Battles of Lexington and Concord, the first major military conflict between British and colonial soldiers. Things were heating up between colonists and the British, and thirty-three-year-old Thomas Ditson, a farmer from Billerica, decided he needed to better arm himself to join the Billerica Minutemen.

Minutemen were regular citizens who agreed to train and, as their name suggests, be ready to go to battle at a minute's notice. They were the rapid response arm of the nascent American military and allowed the colonists to assemble respectably sized forces to defend against British aggressions when and where they happened, rather than having to maintain large dedicated military bodies around the colonies. Most minutemen were young, passionate and dedicated to the fight for freedom. It makes sense, then, that aspiring minuteman Thomas Ditson would want reliable and plentiful guns to take with him into battle.

As the story goes, Ditson went into Boston to sell his crops and procure himself some guns, which was perfectly legal at the time. His plan was to find a British soldier who had guns to sell. This seems like a very counterintuitive move. Why would an American militiaman attempt to buy guns from a British soldier, against whom he would presumably be using those guns? Like, "Hey British soldier, can you sell me a whole bunch of guns to use to shoot at you?" It's pretty bizarre, but apparently, at the time, British soldiers were known to regularly sell off guns and other supplies from the king's stores in order to line their own pockets, so Ditson had every reason to believe this transaction would be unremarkable. Additionally, not having a crystal ball, Ditson couldn't have known that the British were growing wary of the colonists having stores of guns and that just a couple weeks later, the British would storm a farm in Concord where they (correctly) suspected a cache of arms was being held. That action rolled into the Battles of Lexington and Concord and started what we know as the American Revolutionary War.[2]

But again, Ditson didn't know any of that. He just knew he wanted guns and British soldiers were the best way to get them.

Once in Boston, Ditson met up with a British soldier who said he had guns to sell. Ditson went with him to his quarters, where they met up with another British soldier. The soldiers took his money to pay for the guns. Here Ditson's story and the soldiers' stories diverge. Ditson claimed that he asked the soldiers many times if they had the right to sell the arms and if it was legal for him to possess them. According to the soldiers, Ditson made grand claims that he would buy any number of weapons at any price if the soldiers would desert and come with him out into the country. Regardless of what happened in the house, it is certain that Ditson was seized by soldiers and brought to the guardhouse, where he would stay overnight based on an obscure and convolutedly interpreted law having to do with buying arms from a soldier and enticing him to desert.

The next morning, Ditson was awoken and told to strip down to his breeches (knee-length pants). He was painted from head to toe in black tar and then covered with feathers. After this, he was put in a chair on the back of a donkey cart and had a sign hung around his neck reading, "American Liberty, or Democracy exemplified in a villain who attempted to incite one of the soldiers of his Majesty's 47th Regiment to desert and take up arms with rebels against his King and country." (Translated into modern English: "These Liberty/Democracy-loving Americans are the worst—here is a perfect example of what jerks they are. Look at this guy who tried to get a British soldier to desert the British army and fight with him against the Crown. Pfft.")[3]

Forty to fifty British soldiers then walked Ditson through the streets of Boston as they taunted him and sang insulting songs.

"What song did they sing?" you might ask. Well, they sang "Yankee Doodle" (and here's where the story comes full circle). They even added a verse about Ditson:

Yankee Doodle came to town,
For to buy a firelock,
We will tar and feather him,
And so we will John Hancock.[4]

(Clearly, these guys really hated John Hancock, to call him out in this situation he was not remotely involved with. I can imagine Hancock hearing about this and being like, "What the heck? What did I have to do with this? I've never even heard of this Ditson guy… Geez!")

The colonists were horrified to see one of their own abused and humiliated, so a crowd formed, and the British officers sensed that things were about to get ugly. They let Ditson go in order to avoid a brawl, and he made it home to Billerica sticky and feathery but otherwise in good health. Word of this bullying spread and presumably helped fan the flames of colonists' animosity toward the British.

The story that spread throughout Boston area apparently included the part about British soldiers tauntingly singing "Yankee Doodle," for in reaction, the colonists collectively reappropriated it as a song of colonial pride. The lyrics went from the British soldiers' intended meaning—"Hey, look at these ragtag and uncouth colonists—what a bunch of fools!"—to what became our current interpretation of the lyrics: "Heck yeah we're rough around the edges, but we can still kick your fancy-uniform-wearing rear ends!"

Ditson may have endured an awful situation, but he also got his revenge in a quite dramatic way. On April 19, just a little over a month after his tarring and feathering, he and the Billerica Minutemen fired on the British soldiers at the Battles of Lexington and Concord. As anyone who went to elementary school in Massachusetts knows, the colonists defeated the British, forcing them to retreat to Boston. This battle marked the start of the American Revolution. And as hopefully anyone who went to elementary school anywhere knows, the American Revolution led to American independence.[5]

Ditson, "Yankee Doodle" and Billerica are forever linked because of that taunting donkey cart ride through Boston. Without that incident, we wouldn't have the song "Yankee Doodle" (all fifteen-plus verses of it) enmeshed in our history as a rallying song of the American Revolution, and a collective tear would roll down the cheek of every fife and drum corps Revolutionary War reenactor.

Billerica has embraced its "Yankee Doodle" heritage and is officially known as Massachusetts' Yankee Doodle Town. Every September, the town holds a Yankee Doodle Homecoming, which includes New England fair standards like a parade, games, vendors and food. It also, however, includes a colonial minuteman encampment like the one Thomas Ditson would have been a part of and a reenactment of his tarring, feathering and parading through the town.[6]

MORLACCHI CAN CANCAN

We all know the cancan dance from Toulouse-Lautrec artwork, the Moulin Rouge and the 1980s Shop Rite "Can Can Sale" commercial, which is still stuck in my head. The cancan actually started out as something very different and took over one hundred years to become the undies-flashing kick-fest we recognize. And while the cancan was a wholly French invention, it took an Italian ballerina to popularize it in the United States. That ballerina was Giuseppina Morlacchi, and she lived for a time in—you guessed it—Billerica.

Giuseppina Morlacchi was born in Italy and classically trained in the finest ballet school around, La Scala in Milan. She became known as the Peerless Morlacchi both for her exquisite dancing and for her character.[7] At the time, in the mid-1800s, younger and less famous dancers were at the mercy of the theater's ownership and were often taken advantage of. Morlacchi used her position to stand up for those dancers and force those in charge to actually pay them and treat them fairly. By all accounts, she was humble and kind and never got caught up in her fame.[8]

The American cancan, looking decidedly more refined than the French version seen in Toulouse-Lautrec's paintings. *Courtesy of UMASS Lowell Library.*

And famous she was. After just a couple years of dancing in the United States, she was the best known and most sought-after dancer in the country. In 1867, an article in the *New York Evening Transcript* proclaimed:

> *The Great Morlacchi whose power of thoughtful, fanciful dancing—music addressed to the eye—has never been equaled by any artist who has visited the country. She has sparked an excitement among the most cultivated classes of our citizens and everyone wants to see her perform.*[9]

This fame and respect afforded her the unusual power to dictate the style of her own shows and to create her own choreography. One of the dances she chose to make her own and bring to U.S. audiences was the cancan, hence making her America's original cancaneuse (yes, it's a word).

In France, the cancan was bawdy, wild and dominated by a woman nicknamed La Goulue, which translates to the Glutton. La Goulue performed at the famous Moulin Rouge and brought to the stage a sense of mischief and debauchery.[10] She was known for grabbing and slugging down customers' drinks and for her scandalously heart-embroidered undies, which she flashed to the crowd as part of her cancan routine.[11] One of her best-known antics was high-kicking off gentlemen's top hats, much to their surprise and delight. While her star faded and her life ended sadly, presumably due to alcoholism, she is immortalized as the cancan girl in many of Toulouse-Lautrec's famous paintings.[12]

Of course, Morlacchi and La Goulue could not have been more different. When Morlacchi brought the cancan to America, she preserved the high-energy fun of it but let the bawdiness and embroidered knickers remain in Paris. She premiered the new dance in Boston to great acclaim, and the Morlacchi Ballet Troupe went on to travel the country performing the "Grand Gallop Can-Can."[13]

After Morlacchi was done with her cancan phase, the classically trained Italian ballerina joined—wait for it—Buffalo Bill Cody's Wild West Show. How the show's writer and promoter, Ned Buntline, managed to convince the most well-known ballerina in American to join a Wild West show remains a mystery. The gig worked out well for Morlacchi, though, as she gained further renown dancing as a Native American princess named Dove Eye. Furthermore, the show is where she met her future husband, John Baker "Texas Jack" Omohundro.[14] Perhaps the most unlikely couple of the time, the rough-and-tumble cowboy Omohundro and the quiet and graceful Morlacchi traveled together for several years. Their adventure ended when Texas Jack died on the road in Colorado.[15] Morlacchi stopped touring and settled down in her home in Lowell and her country home in Billerica to lead the quiet life she had always wanted. She died just six years later and is buried at Saint Patrick Cemetery in Lowell.[16]

If you've ever seen a cancan performed, the first thing you likely thought was, *Dear Lord, I'd pass out if I tried to do that.* At least, that's what I thought. In order to try to get a more visceral feeling for what performing the cancan is like, I spoke with Veronica Foley, who, despite being a Massachusetts native and a professional dancer, claims to have never seen the Shop Rite Can Can ad.

Me: Veronica, can can you do the cancan?

Veronica: Yes! I can can do the cancan.

Me: Had you responded in any other format, I would have ended this interview right now. Tell me a little about your experience with the cancan.

Veronica: I learned the cancan as a competition dancer at Mary Flynn Murphy School of Dance in Somerville. We competed with a cancan number at a national level. The cancan is exhausting, as it requires high energy to perform. There is a lot of repetitive movement and high kicking, and sometimes a cartwheel is thrown in! The most challenging movement is the high kick transitioning into a split. My second experience was performing a rendition of the cancan during a production of *Cabaret* as one of the Kit Kat Club girls.

Me: That's impressive. So, would you describe yourself as a cancaneuse? I'm going to arbitrarily and with no authority define the requirements for cancaneuse as being able to kick the top hat off a six-foot-tall man, à la La Goulue.

Veronica: Although I do not consider myself a cancaneuse, I would still be able to kick the top hat off a six-foot-tall man, thanks to my training as a young dancer.

Me: As a six-foot-tall woman, I will remember to watch my top hat around you.

Veronica: You should definitely watch it.

Me: Noted.[17]

---

1. Billerica Colonial Minute Men, "Yankee Doodle Story," August 16, 2017, https://bcmm.us.
2. Ibid.
3. Thomas Ditson, "Deposition of Thomas Ditson, Jun. of Billerica, Who Was Tarred and Feathered in Boston, by Order of Col. Nesbit, of His Majesty's Forty-Seventh Regiment," Northern Illinois University Digital Library, https://digital.lib.niu.edu.
4. Billerica Colonial Minute Men, "Yankee Doodle Story," August 16, 2017, https://bcmm.us.
5. Jane L. Green, "Thomas Ditson: Puritan to Bumpkin to Patriot," *Journal of the American Revolution*, February 8, 2022, https://allthingsliberty.com.
6. Billerica's Yankee Doodle Homecoming, https://billericayankeedoodlehomecoming.org/.
7. Wikipedia, "Giuseppina Morlacchi," https://wikipedia.org.
8. Tony Sampas, "Lowell History: Texas Jack and the Peerless Morlacchi," University of Massachusetts Lowell Library, last updated July 8, 2022, https://libguides.uml.edu.
9. Chris Enss, "Wild Women of the West: Giuseppina Morlacchi," *Cowgirl*, April 16, 2019, https://www.cowgirlmagazine.com.

10. Alex Short, "Cancan: The Forgotten History of France's Most Famous Dance," December 10, 2020, *Dance as Cultural Knowledge* (blog), https://danc102f.wescreates.wesleyan.edu.
11. Moulin Rouge, "French Cancan: The Flagship Dance of the Moulin Rouge Show," February 4, 2022, https://www.moulinrouge.fr.
12. Simple English Wikipedia, "La Goulue," https://simple.wikipedia.org.
13. Wikipedia, "Giuseppina Morlacchi," https://wikipedia.org.
14. Chris Enss, "Wild Women of the West: Giuseppina Morlacchi," *Cowgirl*, April 16, 2019, https://www.cowgirlmagazine.com; Austin Stahl, "'Texas Jack' Omohundro Was the World's First Celebrity Cowboy," HistoryNet, February 22, 2023, https://www.historynet.com.
15. HistoryNet, "The Most Popular Dancer of Her Era, She Once Shared the Stage With Buffalo Bill," May 22, 2023, https://www.historynet.com.
16. Wikipedia, "Giuseppina Morlacchi," https://wikipedia.org.
17. Veronica Foley, interview with the author, June 1, 2024.

CHAPTER 17

SCITUATE

Natalia's mom was tired of her running around downtown Scituate with food in her mouth, so she yelled, "**Sit! Chew it!**"

Ghost stories, love stories, notable architecture origin stories and "eccentric zillionaire" stories: these are, of course, some of the best kinds of stories, and Scituate delivered all four. But the gifts of Scituate don't stop there. It turns out the eccentric zillionaire is the one who was in love and the one behind the building. Plus, *he is the ghost*! Kick your feet up and imagine you're soaking up the sun at Hummock Beach as you enjoy these interwoven tales.

LAWSON TOWER

Thomas W. Lawson and Jeannie Lawson are the power couple behind all these great tales. They grew up together just north of Boston, not rich, and Thomas ended up amassing a huge fortune. By all accounts, Thomas truly loved Jeannie. This was not one of those Gilded Age marriages of financial and political alliance; this was a love marriage. For a guy who was apparently a tough businessman and made a lot of enemies, it seems he was a bit of a mush-ball when it came to his wife.

Lawson learned about the stock market as a young whippersnapper working as a clerk in a Boston bank. He had a particular knack for dealing in copper shares, and when a copper boom hit in the late nineteenth century, his personal wealth ballooned, and he achieved millionaire status. Of course, with that much money, one must have an impressive summer home. When on a drive one summer day, Jeannie and Thomas saw a huge parcel of land with many different types of terrain, all leading down to a beautiful ocean view below. Jeannie thought it would be an ideal spot for their home, and Thomas obliged. He bought the land and began the construction of what would become Dreamworld, one of the time's most elaborate and famous country estates.[1]

An article by the Scituate Historical Society, a wealth of information on the Lawsons, quotes writer Maurice Baldwin: "*Aladdin's lamp* would be a poor substitute for Mr. Thomas W. Lawson's checkbook."[2]

That checkbook was about to get another workout when, just as Dreamworld was nearing completion, the Scituate Water Company dared to build a gigantic water tower within its view. The Lawsons had spent so much time and money building this, well, Dreamworld, and now the view was marred by a huge industrial water tank. When I first read that Jeannie was upset by this, I envisioned a spoiled rich lady throwing a fit that something as pedantic as the commoners' need for drinking water should disrupt her view of the ocean. But the more I read about the Lawsons, the less I found that personification fit. Jeannie was apparently very down to earth, caring, supportive of the less fortunate (which, to be fair, was pretty much everyone) and quite a homebody.[3] Thomas was the more bombastic one; if anyone was going to have a fit, it was going to be him. Based on these characterizations, it's more likely that Jeannie expressed sadness that the view was impacted and asked Thomas if he had any ideas about what could be done, and Thomas sprang into action to ameliorate any gloom in the heart of his love.

Presumably, moving the tower was not an option, so Lawson decided the next best thing would be to camouflage it. He sent his architect to Europe to study the design of old (respectable-looking) towers, and the architect returned with a design from a fifteenth-century watchtower from the Rhine River region.[4] The tower/shell was constructed to encase the unsightly water tower, and of course, Lawson's magical checkbook covered the whole bill. But Lawson didn't stop there. Why just have a 150-foot medieval-style

Lawson Tower in Scituate. You'd never know there was a gigantic, ugly metal water tower lurking inside the gorgeous exterior. Image source: *By ToddC4176 via Wikipedia, CC BY-SA 3.0.*

tower to gaze at when you could have a 150-foot medieval-style *bell*tower to gaze at *and* listen to? Lawson commissioned and installed a set of ten massive bells. A case study by the Cedar Shake and Shingle Bureau covering the 2013 restoration of the tower's exterior gives a clear explanation of the bell system. (And how awesome is it that an Eagle Scout candidate helped restore the bell-playing system?!)

> *The Meneely Company of Troy, New York, cast the bells for Lawson Tower in the early 20th Century. Scituate owes a debt of gratitude to Eagle Scout candidate Joe James III. He chose to focus his badge earning service project on restoring the tower's console system that allowed for the bells to be played from the ground level console room via 10 wooden levers, connected to the top of the tower by chains and pulleys. At the apex of the tower are the bells, accessible by circular staircase. Beneath the roof is the clock, for which the largest bell plays on the hour. The largest bell weighs 3,000 pounds and has a diameter of 52.5 inches. The collection of bells peal with 2–8 bells, chime with 9–22 bells and present a carillon when 23 or*

> *more bells play. Currently,* [a volunteer from the Scituate Historical Society] *goes up to the tower once a week to wind the bells so they play at the right time. Today the bells play a delightful medley on special occasions, further reinforcing Lawson Tower's reputation as an important landmark.*[5]

Lawson's Tower is described as "the most beautiful, most photographed, and most expensive water tower in the world" and is on the National Register of Historic Places.[6] In an ironic twist (pay attention, Alanis Morissette), the actual water tower structure that Lawson's contribution was built to disguise is no longer standing inside the "shell." I hope Mrs. Lawson would approve.

THE MRS. THOMAS W. LAWSON CARNATION

…is a heck of a long name for a flower. It's also the foundation for a great story about things insanely rich people do for the people they love.

Let's back up for a second and consider Thomas Lawson as a whole person. The Scituate Historical Society (SHS) has done a great job of compiling insights into him as a human, not just as a financier. An interview Robert Chessia of the SHS gave to Wicked Local indicates that Thomas Lawson was actually a decent person, though known for being tough in business. "He hired locals, gave them houses on his property, allowed them to cut firewood on the land he was clearing….He held parties for the townspeople, especially the Welcome Party after World War II, and the dedication of Lawson Park for the Civil War veterans."[7]

Chessia's interview also offers several other examples of Lawson's good-heartedness. He tried to give away a horse and carriage at the Marshfield Fair (of which he was marshal for fifteen years) and was arrested for running an illegal lottery. His racehorse's winnings were given to charity. During World War I, he was planning to convert Dreamworld to a food processing plant to supply rations to troops.[8]

(There's also a top-notch "spiteful rich guy" story in there: "When Lawson couldn't sail his boat, 'Independence,' in the America's Cup because he was not a member of the New York Yacht Club, he had the boat scrapped. The sail became the cover of his book about the America's Cup. The first copy was sent to the New York Yacht Club.")[9]

It's in the spirit of "Lawson as a person with a good heart" that I like to consider this next story.

Okay, back to that long-named flower. One of the Lawsons' many interests was horticulture, specifically flowers. While carnations are somewhat out of fashion now (sorry, Market Basket floral department), they were all the rage at the turn of the twentieth century.[10] A man named Peter Fisher cultivated a new carnation in a lovely pink shade and sold it to a Mr. Thomas Galvin, a friend of Thomas Lawson's. Galvin appears to have been some sort of international flower baron, owning multiple florist shops in addition to flower farms and even a tobacco farm in Cuba.[11] He named the new carnation in honor of Jeannie, hence the name the Mrs. Thomas W. Lawson Carnation (because God forbid a woman actually be referred to by her own name). The flower became hugely popular across the country due to its gigantic blooms and beautiful color.

Around January 1899, a bidding war began for possession of the Mrs. Thomas W. Lawson Carnation. I can't suss out why Galvin put the flower up for sale or if he never actually did put it up for sale but it was just so popular that he started receiving offers. Regardless, something happened, and rich people were clamoring to get a piece of the Mrs. Thomas W. Lawson Carnation.

Harlow Higinbotham, president of the 1893 Chicago World's Fair, offered Galvin $15,000 for a half share of ownership of the flower. Never to be outdone, Lawson swooped in with an offer of $30,000 for Galvin's entire stock of eight thousand plants. In today's dollars, that's over $1.1 million.[12] Buying the entire stock would also mean that Lawson had a monopoly on the flower. Nobody else could propagate or own the Mrs. Thomas W. Lawson Carnation except for Mr. Thomas W. Lawson.

The bidding war and resulting transaction caused quite the stir both in the flower world and in the, uh, non-flower world. There was such an interest in the matter that Galvin was compelled to take out a nearly half-page ad on page 1 of the *Sunday Boston Globe* in January 1899. The title was "Mrs. Thomas W. Lawson Carnation: Notice to the Public."[13] In it, Galvin explained to the panicked masses that the carnation would remain commercially available and that the "tens of thousands" of inquiries and orders he received would all at least be partially fulfilled. He then went on to publish a letter he and "The Florists Exchange" (presumably a trade group) sent to Thomas Lawson, Mr. Lawson's reply and a letter from Peter Fisher, the flower's originator, clarifying his interests in the flower.[14] The Florist Exchange's letter is straightforward and businesslike, as is Peter Fisher's. Lawson's is, well, not.

Reading Lawson's letter with a straight face is difficult. He is so impassioned about this flower and his language gets so… flowery? First, in explaining his reasoning behind the exorbitant offer, he says, "I made my offer to Mr. Galvin after reading of the attempts of Chicago and New York men to transplant this beautiful flower to one or both of these great hurly-burly modern Babylons."[15] He goes on (remember, talking about a flower), "In my mind's eye I saw this pretty child of nature, typical in its every part of Boston, with its tint of pink, found nowhere but on the cheeks of Boston maidens, cheeks which are nipped in the morning by the crispy breezes from off the Berkshire hills. [He goes on about the Boston maidens' cheeks for at least eight more lines.] …In my mind's eye I saw this child of Boston's nurture torn from those she loved and knew, and who loved and understood her, and taken to Chicago, with its magnified, quick grandeur, its built-by-night palaces, its breezy nobility and its million of blue-ribbon porcine prize winners."[16] This continues.

Eventually, he gets to the part where he says yes, indeed, he bought the whole stock for $30,000 and then explains why it was a brilliant business move. Then he challenges any grower to "grow a carnation finer than the Mrs. Thomas W. Lawson any time before February 1, 1900." If any grower could do so, Lawson offered a $5,000 prize and $30,000 for eight thousand of this new carnation.[17]

The whole thing seems a little unhinged until you remember this flower is named after his wife. Rereading the deeply weird ode to the cheeks of Boston maidens and how horrid he felt when thinking of being dispossessed of the flowery-prose-inspiring flower, it almost sounds like a love note to Jeannie. Maybe Lawson was a little bit of a softie, and maybe he just couldn't bear the idea of the Mrs. Thomas W. Lawson Carnation being left in the care of someone who wouldn't properly treasure her—I mean, it.

Dreamworld's Ghost

Jeannie died at Dreamworld in 1906, when the youngest of her six children was just nine years old.[18] She and Lawson had known each other since childhood and been married twenty-eight years, and he was utterly gutted by her death.[19] He was unable to keep up his business acumen, potentially due to grief, and lost his fortune, dying nearly penniless. He had to watch his and Jeannie's beloved Dreamworld auctioned off to pay debts in 1922, and he died just three years later. This formerly larger-than-life man must have died truly heartbroken.

After Dreamworld was auctioned off, it became a function hall, hosting weddings and other events. A 2019 *Patriot Ledger* article featured Moira Ward, daughter of Dreamworld Hall's former owner. She and her siblings grew up running around Dreamworld while their dad was working. According to Ward, despite it being beautiful, "Dreamworld was spooky. None of us liked to be there alone. There was something about it; it was a feeling….It was scary….We felt like we were being watched."[20] Ward recounted several creepy stories—windows opening and closing, lights going on and off—but this one takes the cake:

> *There was no one there but us. My father was talking to the man he was walking around with. I was standing six feet away. I remember there was this big heavy door to the cocktail lounge. I was standing at this door. It probably weighed several hundred pounds. This door swung open and this green cloud in the shape of a man, an oval shape, went right past us. And it was cold. You could feel it. It was cold. I was knocked senseless.*[21]

Robert Chessia of the Scituate Historical Society was interviewed for the same article about ghost encounters.

> *My aunt and a friend were in Mrs. Lawson's room when the door slammed shut locking them in the room. After a while it opened by itself and they were able to get out. They never went back.*[22]

The consensus among those who experienced the ghost was that it was Mr. Lawson. "It was his house. He loved that place," Ward said. "I felt like he was saying, 'Hi, I'm here and this is still my house.'"[23]

The building was converted to condos in the 1980s, and Chessia says he hasn't heard of any ghost sightings since then. Maybe Lawson was upset that his home, where he raised six kids with his beloved wife, was being used as a party venue. Maybe now he is at rest knowing that Dreamworld is once again a home.

---

1. Scituate Historical Society, "Lawson Gates," https://scituatehistoricalsociety.org.
2. Ibid.
3. *Boston Globe*, "Mrs. Thomas W. Larson Dead at Dreamworld," August 6, 1906.
4. Scituate Historical Society, "Lawson Tower," https://scituatehistoricalsociety.org.

5. Lynne Christensen, *Lawson Tower: a View with A Thrill*, February 2013, Cedar Shake and Shingle Bureau, http://www.cedarbureau.org; Scituate Historical Society, "Lawson Tower," https://scituatehistoricalsociety.org.
6. Scituate Historical Society, "Lawson Tower," https://scituatehistoricalsociety.org.
7. Ruth Thompson, "Scituate Back in Time: 20 Fun Facts about Thomas Lawson," Wicked Local, https://www.wickedlocal.com.
8. Ibid.
9. Ibid.
10. Glorist, "A Brief History of Carnations: The Meaning, History, and Symbolism of the Flower," June 15, 2023, https://gloristflowers.com.
11. *The Successful American* (Press Biographical Company, 1899).
12. *Arizona Republic*, "A Small Fortune for Pinks," January 26, 1899; *Boston Globe*, "Mrs. Thomas W. Lawson Carnation," January 29, 1899.
13. *Boston Globe*, "Mrs. Thomas W. Lawson Carnation," January 29, 1899.
14. Ibid.
15. Ibid.
16. Ibid.
17. Ibid.
18. *Boston Globe*, "Mrs. Thomas W. Larson Dead at Dreamworld," August 6, 1906.
19. Ruth Thompson, "A Dreamworld Haunting," *Patriot Ledger*, https://www.patriotledger.com.
20. Ibid.
21. Ibid.
22. Ibid.
23. Ibid.

CHAPTER 18

THE HAMS

The settlers in Stoneham's favorite punishment for a thief was to **stone 'em**. The more verbose settlers in Chatham preferred to **chat 'em** to death. The Needham folks said just throw them out in the wilderness; we don't **need 'em**. Their buddies in Dedham agreed any was a sure way to **dead 'em**.

There are nineteen hams in Massachusetts. Here they are, in no particular order: Chatham, Stoneham, Wareham, Dedham, Needham, Hingham, Framingham, Petersham, Bellingham, Ashburnham, Raynham, Wilbraham, Wrentham, Eastham, Wenham, Pelham, Tyringham, Waltham and Oakham.

So what's up with all the hams? Edgar B. Herwick III of WGBH's Curiosity Desk addressed this question in 2022.

> *That "ham" itself—in old English means "home," which is why it sort of doubles to mean "village" as well. So that word "ham" actually means home.…So when you have something like Stoneham, for example, likely there was a village which was a home to people which was probably near a stone somewhere that got called "stone ham."*[1]

Makes sense.

Okay, then why are some pronounced *ham* and some *humm*? Herwick also addressed that in a Facebook video for WGBH. But he called in the big guns. Charles Chang, a linguistics professor from Boston University, explained that whether a town is a ham or a humm depends on a thing called a stress clash. A stress clash occurs when two strong syllables are back-to-back, and English speakers like to avoid it. He gave the example of Needham. *Need* is a strong syllable, as is *ham*. So Needham, with the *ham* pronounced like the food, is awkward due to a stress clash, and we soften the *ham* to a *humm*. On the flip side, he shows that Petersham has a strong *Pe* and then a soft *ters*, which makes it easy to say *ham*, like the food. Of course, Massachusetts is a state full of contrarian Yankees, so we have to throw in exceptions. Waltham, Wareham and Eastham fit the bill.[2]

All the hams, like the boroughs (see chapter 19), have great stories to offer, so to save you from lugging around a thirty-pound book, I had to pick and choose. I'll tell you a few shorter stories and a couple longer ones.

NORUMBEGA

Norumbega is a land "discovered" by several early explorers to the New World, said to lie along the coast of New England. David Ingram, a fifteenth-century shipwrecked English sailor,

> *saw kings decorated with rubies six inches long; and they were borne on chairs of silver and crystal, adorned with precious stones. He saw pearls as common as pebbles, and the natives were laden down by their ornaments of gold and silver. The city of Bega was three-quarters of a mile long and had many streets wider than those of London. Some houses had massive pillars of crystal and silver.*[3]

The way Norumbega was mapped would put it somewhere in Maine-ish, but over time, people figured out the city wasn't really there. A cabal of WASPy Bostonians, however, desperately wanted to say the legend of Norumbega was actually about Vinland, a North American Viking settlement from the eleventh century. Vinland was recorded in the travel logs of Leif Erikson, but nobody knew for sure where it was. But if Leif Erikson was actually the first White guy to set foot in North America, that would mean that a fellow (tenuously) Protestant Northern European guy

A very detailed map for a place that doesn't exist. *Courtesy of Andy Woodruff, https://andywoodruff.com.*

was the real deal, not that swarthy Italian guy, Christopher Columbus. With an influx of Catholic immigrants, these Boston Brahmins were looking to assert that indeed it was their kind that settled North America, not the immigrants' kind. One of the Boston Brahmins was Needham's own William Baker. (Yes, this is all really confusing. To really understand it, you need a whiteboard and Dr. Gloria Greis of the Needham History Center & Museum. And buckle up, 'cause it's gonna get weirder.)

The person really leading the charge, though, was a Harvard chemistry professor named Eben Horsford. Horsford had invented double-acting baking powder (the same stuff we use today) and became fabulously rich. He really wanted Leif Erikson to unseat Columbus, so much so that he conducted "archaeological digs," including one in Cambridge that supposedly unearthed Erikson's original settlement. He published all sorts of "proof" that Ericson was the true discoverer of North America and eventually got enough people on board that in 1885, a huge statue of Leif Erikson "discovering North America" was erected on Commonwealth Avenue in Boston. The base is inscribed, "Leif the Discoverer, Son of Erik, who sailed from Iceland and landed on this continent, AD 1000." Um, no. No, he didn't. Eventually, the statue was moved from its original location to the westernmost end of the Comm Ave parkway. It's a beautiful statue from an artistic standpoint but just so ragingly bizarre from a historical one.

OLD SHIP CHURCH

Seema, the Indian spice enthusiast and gum maker from Hingham, loved the oniony, garlicky taste of hing. She was disappointed to find that there wasn't much of a market for her new product, **hing gum**.

Hingham boasts many beautiful and well-preserved colonial-era buildings, perhaps none so important as the Old Ship Church. The church was built in 1681 as both a place of worship and a town meetinghouse, and it is the only seventeenth-century meetinghouse left in the country. It is also the oldest continually in use house of worship in the country, currently housing a Unitarian congregation. Both the interior and the exterior are stunning. It's awe-inspiring to imagine that the church was built entirely by hand, from trees felled with axes and dragged to the site. Behind the church, as with most old New England churches, is a graveyard, also dating from the seventeenth century. Paul Revere's daughter is one of the notable people buried there.[4] The Old Ship Church also has a prominent standing in New York City. Huh? In fact, the Meetinghouse Gallery in the Metropolitan Museum of Art's American Wing was actually designed as an interior replica of the church. The gallery houses the museum's collection of American paintings and furniture from 1650 to 1720, featuring these pieces in a setting contemporary to them—what better design could there be?[5] So next time you're in Hingham, or New York City, you will have

Nineteenth-century postcard of the Old Ship Church. *Courtesy of the New York Public Library.*

the chance to see an incredible example of seventeenth-century American architecture.

SACCO AND VANZETTI

Dedham has so many wonderful things to offer. My favorite ice cream shop (Ron's) and my favorite kids' bookstore (Blue Bunny) are right next to each other on High Street. The Dedham Museum & Archive offers great exhibits and always warrants a visit. But Dedham's courthouse was the site of one of the most flagrantly racist/anti-immigrant perversions of justice in U.S. history. Nicola Sacco and Bartolomeo Vanzetti were Italian immigrants and members of the anarchist movement. These were not anarchists like '80s punk anarchists who went around spray-painting big red circle-As on buildings. They were everyday people who believed that institutions, including governments, held too much unchecked power over the common people. There were extremists, but those were in the minority. Sacco and Vanzetti were arrested for the armed robbery of $15,000 from a Braintree, Massachusetts shoe company and the murder of a payroll clerk and a security guard during that robbery. The evidence was spurious at best, and the judge let the prosecution run wild with unrelated immigrant-based fear-mongering. The jury convicted them, and the judge refused any appeals.[6] They were executed despite massive protests. The case remains a prime example of what tragedies can occur when prejudices infiltrate the judiciary.

Mourners follow the hearses with the remains of Sacco and Vanzetti through Boston.

ALICE STALLKNECHT

The Chatham Historical Society runs the Atwood Museum, a historical house that houses its extensive collections. Alice Stallknecht was a Chatham-based artist who painted the striking murals at the museum. The subject matter is "the ethos of Chatham in the 1930s," as the murals were painted in that turbulent decade. There are many notable artists with links to Chatham, but Alice Stallknecht struck me because of this quote from her self-written bio on the CHS's site:

> *Like many aspiring female artists, before and since, I found myself overwhelmed by the responsibilities and trials of domestic life that Germaine Greer described in* The Obstacle Race: The Fortune of Women Painters and Their Work.[7]

She then goes on to describe how she helped get her son established as an artist and took a mural class at the art school he attended. She then traveled to Europe with him.

> *It was after I returned from Europe that I began to develop my own work. By then I was in my forties, my son was raised, my husband was gainfully employed, and I had both the time and the money to paint. During these years I produced three life-size portraits of the American presidents.... The size of these portraits was the first indication that I was attempting to paint on the scale of murals, which inspired me to paint the three murals now on display in the Mural Barn at the Atwood Museum.*[8]

Most women who raise children while either working outside the home or trying to pursue artistic aspirations, even these days, can relate to the first quote and hope for the second. From the 1910s to the 1930s, Alice Stallknecht grappled with this challenge and overcame it in grand fashion, as is apparent when looking at the powerful figures and scale of the CHS murals.[9] Stallknecht piqued my interest because of her ability to articulate this difficulty in a time when a woman's artistic pursuits were largely considered folly relative to her role as a mother. She then blew me away by how boldly she burst forth from these constraints, creating massive, unapologetic murals asserting her artistic prowess.

Alice Stallknecht at work. You need a massive paint palette to support a massive talent. *Courtesy of Cape Cod Community College Nickerson Archives.*

ZooLights!

The Stone Zoo's annual ZooLights! draws thousands of people, many of whom went every year as kids and now bring their kids. It began when a Christmas-loving Peabody couple, Arthur "Skip" and Shirley LaBrie, were

Some goofy kids enjoying ZooLights! at the Stone Zoo. *Author's collection.*

moving and needed to relocate the holiday display they'd had at their home for many years.[10] By this point, the LaBries needed a police detail to manage the traffic as people visited the wonderland they created and added to every year.[11] The LaBries included in their display a wishing well and fountain that visitors would throw coins into and donated all the proceeds to local charities.[12] The Stone Zoo proved the perfect place to receive their Christmas decoration bonanza of a donation. In 1996, the first ZooLights! took place, bringing in thousands of visitors. The cold-hardy animals, of which there are many at the Stone Zoo, were on display in their outside enclosures, and many warm-weather animals were also on display in appropriate quarters. Visitors could have their picture taken with the reindeer, visit Santa and, of course, stroll around and look at the hundreds of thousands of lights and lighted displays. Over time, the event's popularity exploded; one year, it attracted sixty thousand people.[13] ZooLights! continues to be a popular Christmastime destination and is a beloved tradition for many families, all because of the love of Christmas and the generosity of one couple.

OCTAGON HOUSES

Octagonal houses were a thing in the 1850s. An "amateur architect" named Orson Fowler (please note: never hire an "amateur architect") popularized them, and scores were built all over the United States and Canada between the 1850s and the turn of the next century.

Fowler was a professional phrenologist (please note: never hire any phrenologist) and is one of the people largely credited for the popularity of phrenology in the mid-1800s. For those of you not well-versed in Victorian-era medical fads, phrenology was the pseudoscientific study of the bumps on people's heads, with the belief that they could be "read" to determine an individual's true nature. This would have been fine if it were just for party games and giggles, but phrenological reports were sometimes used to justify committing individuals to asylums and presented as evidence at trial to support the claim that a defendant was naturally predisposed to committing crimes. Phrenology also asserted that African and Jewish people's head bumps exposed them as unintelligent and deceitful, respectively. Women's head bumps were a dead giveaway that they were unfit for the study of the arts and sciences (which is weird because Fowler was also a staunch advocate of women's rights).[14]

Fowler's influence went beyond head bumps, and he took on a sort of early influencer role in Victorian society. He authored a book titled *The Octagon House: A Home for All*, which extolled the virtues of living in an octagon house and explained the benefits in efficiency and square-footage maximization. He built an octo-mansion (not a real word) to prove his point:

> *To illustrate and justify the technical and ideological proposals that the book outlined, Fowler built a magnificent octagonal house for his family in Fishkill, New York. The house had four floors and sixty rooms and forty other miscellaneous rooms and closets. At the center stood a spiral staircase that rose seventy feet to a glass enclosed octagonal cupola. Each floor was encircled by a porch that went all the way around. The house had central heating, running water, indoor flush toilets, a roof cistern to collect rain water, natural gas lighting, and a water filtration system. There were speaking tubes for inter-communication between the various rooms, and dumbwaiters to bring foods from the kitchen in the basement to the dining room.*[15]

People were way into it.

The William Bryant octagon house at 12 Spring Street is considered the best preserved of the four octagon houses in Stoneham. Bryant was a shoe cutter, part of Stoneham's large shoemaking industry at the time.

Stoneham's Enoch Fuller octagon house at 72 Pine Street has been lovingly referred to for generations as the "birthday cake house."[16] It is the only one of the Stoneham octagons to have a flying staircase, a wrapping central staircase designed such that someone could stand in the middle of the house and look all the way straight up to see the cupola.

A slight aside: The flying staircase is surely a beautiful architectural feature but also, shall we say, not the safest design choice. A 1969 article in the *Boston Globe* speaks of an octagon house in Washington, D.C., that is supposedly haunted by three girls, all of whose deaths somehow involved the flying staircase. The original owner's eldest daughter ran up the stairs after a fight with her father, who disapproved of the man she wanted to marry. She crashed through the second-floor banister and fell to her death. The same man, who apparently hadn't learned much from the loss of his eldest daughter, had a fight with his second daughter over another marriage

One of the four octagon houses still standing in Stoneham. *Author's collection.*

arrangement. He shoved her, and she fell backward over the banister and plummeted to the ground, where she broke her neck and died. Lastly, an enslaved woman was thrown from the top floor by a British naval officer she refused to marry. He then jumped to his death immediately after realizing what he had done. According to the *Globe* article, the house is now haunted by these spirits.[17]

To the best of my knowledge, thankfully, nobody ever died falling from (or being pushed off) the flying staircase in the Fuller House. But to anyone who goes in there: please watch your step.

Flying staircase aside, the Fuller octagon house is the most elaborate of the four. It also has a cool origin story.

Per the National Register of Historic Places record:

> *Mr. Fuller was a friend of P.T. Barnum, of the circus Barnum and Bailey. Fuller reportedly stayed in Barnum's Bridgeport Connecticut octagon, and was impressed with the design. Fuller's role in Stoneham history is not clear: he did not live in the house very long, and it served as a boarding house by 1858. The owner at that time was Benjamin Goldsmith. By 1874 it was owned by G.W. Trowbridge, manufacturer of shoe tips.*[18]

While Victorian-era Stonehamites (Stonehamians?) clearly loved their octagons, another group of people took their octagonal passions to extremes. A group of vegetarian utopian idealists attempted to found a colony in Kansas based on their principles. Their leader, a famous vegetarian-lifestyle advocate named Henry S. Clubb, believed in the ideas put forth by Fowler in his book and planned the settlement to be based on eights. The town square would be an octagon, and it would have eight radiating roads, each of which would lead to eight (presumably octagonal) farmhouses with octagonal barns. In a fit of unbridled creativity, the settlement was called Octagon City. The octo-plan never came to fruition, and the octo-settlers never made it through even one octo-winter. (I'll stop. Stop-tagon.)[19]

Luckily, the octagon houses in Stoneham have remained occupied and well cared for over the years. You can take a little drive around town and check them out. They're private residences, though, so don't do anything creepy, like knock on the doors and try to get the owners to move to Kansas with you to start a vegetarian idealist utopia.

THE BAKER ESTATE

When I emailed with Dr. Gloria Greis, executive director of the Needham History Center & Museum, she kindly sent me links to some particularly interesting stories from the museum's blog. One of the stories was about goings-on at the Baker Estate, and she added the comment, "There is no shortage of stories about the Baker Estate." Wow. She wasn't kidding.

The Baker Estate was the summer home of William Emerson Baker, who made his fortune via his sewing machine company, Baker & Grover. At age forty, Emerson retired. This was in 1868, during the "robber baron" era, when there weren't a ton of laws regulating business dealings and a small number of men were able to amass revoltingly huge fortunes. (Think Newport mansion money.) So here was Baker, richer than several small nations and with no pesky job to occupy his days. What to do, what to do…

There are many reasons people wish to be rich. Personally, I see it as carte blanche for absolute eccentricity. Walk your pack of pet chipmunks down the streets of New York accompanied by a guy with a '90s boom box blasting Indigo Girls? Sure, why not. You're rich. Show up at a party in a sixteen-foot-tall hat made of shaving cream with candy cane scaffolding? Yup. Sounds good. You're rich. Of course, it's also an opportunity to help people and the world, but if you're really rich, you have the leeway to accomplish that in a totally bananas manner. That's what William Baker did.

When the Civil War ended, there was great concern about how to reunite the North and the South. Officially, of course, that had been accomplished by treaties and other legalities. But the people of the North and South were, understandably, still bitterly divided and saw each other as enemies. This was a problem politically and socially but also from a business perspective for folks like Baker. He wanted to be able to sell his wares in as many markets as possible, and North/South tensions could make that difficult. About ten years after the end of the Civil War, Baker was in Charleston, South Carolina, and met with members of the Washington Light Infantry, who fought for the Confederacy. The meeting apparently went well, for after he returned to Massachusetts, he received a gift from them: a cannon.

When one receives a cannon as a gift, one must throw a party. Baker installed the cannon on a hill and invited the Washington Light Infantry up to Needham for a soiree to celebrate. He also invited various Massachusetts dignitaries, making the guest list a mix of Northerners and Southerners. The invitation, referencing the cannon, read, "You who stood behind it, will meet those who stood in front of it, and shake hands over it."[20] My initial reaction to reading this was that this could go one of two ways: badly or really badly. Instead, it went fantastically.

The party lasted a full week. They drank, they danced, they drank some more. Then, as Greis writes,

> *Toward the end, the Southerners gathered noisemakers, drums, pots and pans and serenaded the ladies with their terrible music. Coming to the rescue, the Northerners ambushed them with pillows obtained from the ladies' quarters. The Southern ladies armed their own men in similar fashion, and a battle between the Blue and Grey Pillow Brigades carried on for over 30 minutes, until innumerable pillows were destroyed, and everyone was laughing too hard to stand.*[21]

Did you catch that? It was a pillow fight—like, a fifth-grade sleepover pillow fight, former Union soldiers and dignitaries versus former Confederate soldiers and dignitaries, people who hated each other from the pitch of their being now united over silliness, seeing the humanity in each other and giving a modicum of hope to the notion of North/South reunification. Remember that thing I said about how when you're really rich you can do good for the world in a really bananas manner? Yeah. Mic drop.

Hang on, I'm picking up that mic again for another story.

Baker had eight hundred acres in Needham to use however he wanted, and what he wanted was fun. Over time, he installed an underground crystal grotto, a pleasure lake, saloons, restaurants, a 225-room luxury hotel, a museum of industry and a zoo.[22] In the zoo were both exotic animals and commonplace animals and—integral to this tale—two bear pits. Baker had several black bears, mostly the older and more chill variety. They hung out, ate their food, napped and did other bear things (like more eating and napping). At one point, Baker decided he wanted to add some younger blood to the mix and purchased two black bear cubs, which would be transported down from Boston's North End. Sadly, one of the little cubs died on the way.

Shortly after, a showman who had a two-year-old male bear that had become too difficult to manage contacted Baker. Baker offered to buy the bear, whose name was Billy Bruin. Billy was transported by train. Baker's handlers were supposed to meet the Billy at the depot and bring him back to the bear pit on the estate. The handlers went on to execute a multilevel fail that led to disaster.

First, they didn't get Billy from the depot on the day he arrived, so he had to stay in his presumably tiny cage at the busy train depot overnight. That had to be stressful for the bear. Then they finally got him back to the estate and, for some reason, didn't put him in the bear pit (which would have given him room to roam a bit and would have properly enclosed him) but chained him to a tree. Now the poor bear had been in a tiny cage on a train for who knows how long, left at a train depot in that cage, presumably transported in a buggy and chained to a tree: peak bear stress achieved. At this point, Baker came down to check out his new bear. His two dogs came with him. When Billy saw the dogs, he freaked out, lunged and broke free from the tree. Baker told the handlers to stay and try to keep Billy contained while he himself ran to try to get something to recapture the bear. The handlers weren't paid enough to stand guard over a supposedly five-hundred-pound, eight-foot-tall, angry young bear, so they high-tailed it out of there. Billy was free.

For the record, the length of time between when Baker's handlers took possession of Billy and when Billy escaped? Three hours. Good job, guys.[23]

The poor bear must have been a mess. He found a safe hiding place under the Dedham Congregational Church porch and slept there for the night. Still dragging his broken chain, he began wandering about the woods in town, dined (unwelcome) at a pig farm, ambled over to Quincy and made his way down to Weymouth. Baker had men out trying to bait him with sugar cubes and even with the sounds of the baby bear Baker had recently acquired. Ten days later, either he drowned or some jerk shot him while he was trying to swim across a river (conflicting accounts exist). His body eventually washed up and was returned to Baker.[24]

That part is unequivocally sad. Then things get twenty-first-century weird and nineteenth-century funny. If it happened today, Baker's next move would be considered somewhere in the vortex of distasteful, miscalculated, disturbing, macabre and, at best, uncomfortably bemusing. In 1874, however, it was just flat-out hilarious. So let's roll with that.

Baker had Billy mounted (the nice word for "stuffed") and the rest of him buried in a copper coffin overlooking a picturesque lake, which I like to think was a sign of respect. Then he used Billy's passing as reason to have a massive funeral for the bear. And by massive, we're talking over one thousand invited guests. Invitees who had the gall to decline an invitation to a bear funeral were asked to send their regrets in the form of a poem, and those poems were bound into books and given as favors to attendees.

From the *Wellesley Townsman*'s December 3, 2015 article on the funeral:

> *The funeral kicked off that day with the arrival of hundreds of Baker's friends at the Wellesley depot. There they were met by a fleet of vehicles that would bring them to Ridge Hill Farms, including horse-drawn phaetons, a jaunting car, a large boat on wheels, as well as an omnibus that was filled with young women dressed in full mourning outfits.*
>
> *Once at the Baker property, a large funeral procession was formed on the Conservatory Lawn (at the current site of 380 Grove Street in Needham). But this wasn't your typical procession. Rather, it was comprised almost entirely of people wearing elaborate costumes that in some way, shape, or form were puns or (attempted) humorous references to bears and Billy Bruin's notorious escape.*
>
> *What follows is a partial list of the participants: the Grand Marshall (Baker) a la cheval, the stuffed corpse of Billy Bruin on a bier carried by four men wearing animal skins to represent the Bulls and Bears of the Financial District, 5-month-old bear cub Topsy, the 20-piece Natick Cornet Band, men dressed as frogs to symbolize the greenbacks of American finance, someone dressed as a monkey as a nod to the wise heads who thought they knew how to catch Billy, Native American hunters, a "black man turned white with bare fright," and following up at the rear, a handful of babies that supposedly had been swallowed by the bear.*[25]

Okay, look. I know that in 150 years, people will look back on us and think we did bizarre things. I'm not ignorant of the fact that history is a harsh

This picture from Billy Bruin's funeral feels ripe for a caption contest. I'll just let you come up with your own. *Courtesy of the J. Paul Getty Museum.*

judge, and the context of a time vastly changes the meanings of actions and events. But Victorians? Come on. So strange.

After this funeral procession, guests (still in their costumes) ate and drank and generally partied. And thus the short life and the long funeral of poor Billy Bruin both came to a close.

It's not fair, however, to end the story of William Emerson Baker on that note. He was a nut who loved a party, but he was also an innovative man who was a generous philanthropist and ahead of his time in many more ways than just party themes. Among the many causes he worked for was public health.

Remember, this is the late nineteenth century. The industrial revolution was in full swing, and what we now consider basic human rights in the workplace and in the home were not yet standard. Indoor plumbing was in its infancy and far from commonplace. Hand-washing was essentially nonexistent, and antibiotics wouldn't be invented for decades.[26] People were trying to figure out how to feed the large workforces gathered in cities when farms could be far away, and food safety was just starting to come into question. In short, it was pretty gross.

Baker recognized that advancements in the (new) field of public health would be necessary to keep the population healthy. To that end, he set up a "piggery" that operated under what were considered radical sanitary conditions. The idea was that if pigs were fed well and kept in clean living conditions, pork would be healthier for the humans who consumed it. He hoped that the innovations he set forth in this piggery would spread for the benefit of all people. And to honor the establishment of the piggery, he had—you guessed it—a gigantic, ridiculous party.

The invitation, which looks more like a booklet than a typical invitation, proclaims:

> *Historic porcine songs will be wanted to be sung by quartette and chorus at the ceremonies attending the laying of the cornerstone of the new piggery, near the banks of the Charles River, which is to be occupied among others, by some of our unimproved Hoggish-English-cousins.*[27]

I'm not sure how many historic songs there are about pigs, but I'm guessing Baker put someone to the task of unearthing all of them.

Though we've momentarily deviated back into the realm of the frivolous, the point here is that Baker combined his penchant for the absurd with truly good works. In fact, upon his death in 1888, most newspapers chose to memorialize him by listing these absurdities. Letters to the editor came in rebuttal to these write-ups, including this one from the *Boston Herald* of January 7, 1888:

> *It is true he had a love of humor and a passion for the grotesque, at times so prodigal and unreserved in their manifestations as not unnaturally to mislead those who could judge only by their appearances. But behind all this there was in him the stuff of which noble hearts and true men are made. If he had a passion for some trifles, he also had a passion for many great and good things.*
>
> *He was one of the most public spirited of men. He had a desire, almost impetuous, to improve the condition of the poor, especially in reference to food and dwellings, and he expended time, money and superabundant labor in endeavoring to perfect and carry out schemes to ameliorate their condition. Not only in these particulars, but in others, which many will recall, he strove to make the life of the poor smoother and better, and to establish institutions of philanthropy and learning. He was one of the first, if not the very first, to suggest the Institute of Technology, and was one of its most ardent friends. There was hardly any limit either to his charitable projects or efforts.*[28]

This reminiscence on the life of William Emerson Baker reminds us that just because someone is goofy and likes a good time, it doesn't mean they can't also be intelligent and good-hearted.

---

1. Edgar B. Herwick III, Paris Alston and Jeremy Siegel, "Why Do So Many Massachusetts' Town Names End in 'Ham'?" WGBH, April 28, 2022, https://www.wgbh.org.
2. Ibid.; "Why Do So Many Mass. Towns End in 'Ham'—and When Do You Pronounce Them 'Ham' or 'Uhm'?" GBH News (Facebook), https://www.facebook.com.
3. Andy Woodruff, "Norumbega, New England's Lost City of Riches and Vikings," *Cartographer* (blog), May 24, 2010, https://andywoodruff.com.
4. Old Ship Church, "History," http://oldshipchurch.org.

5. Constance Gorfinkle, "Hingham's Old Ship Meeting House Inspires Metropolitan Museum of Art Gallery," *Patriot Ledger*, May 16, 2009, https://www.patriotledger.com.
6. Massachusetts Court System, "Sacco & Vanzetti: Justice on Trial, at the John Adams Courthouse," https://www.mass.gov.
7. Alice Stallknecht, "Alice Stallknecht: Mural Artist," Atwood Museum, https://chathamhistoricalsociety.org.
8. Ibid.
9. Linda Botsford and Deborah Ecker, "Alice Stallknecht's Mural Paintings," Atwood Museum, https://chathamhistoricalsociety.org.
10. John Laidler, "ZooLights Illuminates Stone Zoo with Holiday Cheer," *Boston Globe*, November 28, 2020, https://www.bostonglobe.com.
11. Rich Fahey, "Lighting Up My Life on Christmas," *Boston Globe*, https://epaper.bostonglobe.com.
12. Conway, Cahill-Brodeur Funeral Home, "Shirley M. LaBrie Obituary," December 29, 2020, https://ccbfuneral.com.
13. Rich Fahey, "Lighting Up My Life on Christmas," *Boston Globe*, https://epaper.bostonglobe.com.
14. Wikipedia, "Orson Squire Fowler," https://wikipedia.org.
15. Kaushik Patowary, "The Octagon Houses of Orson Fowler," Amusing Planet, March 10, 2021, https://www.amusingplanet.com.
16. Richard Powers, "Stoneham Back Where It Started—and Likes It That Way," *Boston Globe*, June 7, 1961.
17. Jacqueline Lawrence, "Three Girls Haunt Washington's Famed Octagon House," *Boston Globe*, October 26, 1969.
18. Massachusetts Historical Commission MACRIS: Massachusetts Cultural Resource Information System, https://mhc-macris.net.1.
19. Atlas Obscura, "Sad Saga of Vegetarian Creek," August 22, 2023, http://www.atlasobscura.com.
20. Gloria Greis, "Needham History: 'To the Departed Spirits'—Remembering the 800-Acre Baker Estate," Wicked Local, May 3, 2021, https://www.wickedlocal.com.
21. Gloria Greis, "Needham History: 'To the Departed Spirits'—Remembering the 800-Acre Baker Estate," Wicked Local, May 3, 2021, https://www.wickedlocal.com.
22. Gloria Greis and Needham History Center & Museum, "Needham History: Good Times at the Baker Estate," Wicked Local, March 23, 2020, https://www.wickedlocal.com.

23. Gloria Greis, "Needham History: 'To the Departed Spirits'—Remembering the 800-Acre Baker Estate," Wicked Local, May 3, 2021, https://www.wickedlocal.com.
24. Ibid.; Josh, "Billy Bruin and His Festive Funeral," *Wellesley History* (blog), October 16, 2016, https://wellesleyhistory.wordpress.com.
25. Josh, "Billy Bruin and His Festive Funeral," *Wellesley History* (blog), October 16, 2016, https://wellesleyhistory.wordpress.com.
26. Global Handwashing Partnership, "History," March 19, 2015, https://globalhandwashing.org.
27. Dan Hinchen, "Porcineographs and Piggeries: William Baker Emerson and Ridge Hill Farms," *Beehive* (blog), the Massachusetts Historical Society, August 1, 2015, https://www.masshist.org.
28. Massachusetts Historical Society, "Object of the Month: Celebrating the Bunker Hill Centennial (and a New Piggery!) At Ridge Hill Farms, 20 June 1875," June 2021, https://www.masshist.org.

CHAPTER 19

THE BOROUGHS/BOROS

When Marley the gopher's mom saw the fox in Marlborough, she yelled "**Marl! Burrow!**"

Marl didn't know which way to go, so his mom yelled, "**West! Burrow!**" and to nobody's surprise, they ended up in Westborough.

The fox was still tracking them, so Marley yelled, "**South! Burrow!**" They got all turned around and started burrowing north instead, which, oddly, landed them in the center of Southborough.

With the fox still on their trail, Marley's mom decided the only safe place was her sister Ting's place in Tyngsborough, so they kept going north and, after hours, ended up busting through the dirt wall of Aunt **Ting's burrow**.

There are eleven boroughs in Massachusetts, which could also be boros. There is only one boro that can't be a borough. While we're at it, a burrow is a hole made by an animal for shelter, and a burro is a small donkey used as a pack animal. The borough/boros (that may also contain burrows and/or burros) in question are, in no particular order: Westborough, Southborough, Middeborough, Northborough, Boxborough, Tyngsborough, Marlborough, Foxborough, Lanesborough,

North Attleborough and New Marlborough. The boro that's not also a borough is Attleboro.

Man, now I need a nap.

And hey Attleboro, thanks for keeping it simple for us. Mayor Cathleen DeSimone explained in a 2023 interview with WBZ News that Attleboro officially designated itself a boro and not a borough in 1914. "I'd like to think Attleboro is ahead of the game, way ahead of the game, and they should try to catch up to us. We innovate, we move and shake." And in reference to the shorter spelling, she says, "I probably save at least 10 minutes a year! So I can take a longer lunch, a little longer walk."[1] Quick note to Mayor DeSimone: Anyone who uses the expression "move and shake" is A+ in my book.

So if the movers and shakers of Attleboro can make the call, then why? *Why?* Why must this added level of complexity exist in an already-too-complex world? Well, at least there is some logic behind it. As we know, early American settlers were a wildly uncreative bunch. If I had the opportunity to name a town, I'd name it something awesome. But no. Apparently too busy fighting off wild animals, making fire and foraging for berries, the settlers just named the new towns after the towns they were from in (mostly) England. Booo-riiing.

In England, there was no "-oro" ending. It was always "-orough." Peter Drummey of the Massachusetts Historical Society, in the same WBZ article as Mayor DeSimone's interview, explains that *borough* was an old English word for a walled-off, self-governed community. (Aside: Does "walled-off, self-governed community" sound kinda like a cult to anyone else?) When settlers came here and named their towns boroughs, there was no reason to spell it differently. Then, in the early 1800s, the *oro* started appearing to save space on official maps and documents.[2]

This is all happening at a time when spelling in American English was not standardized. If you look at old journals from the seventeenth and eighteenth centuries, you might see an individual spelling the same word different ways even in the same entry. Even founding father types, who were mostly as highly educated as one could be at the time, used spelling that looks all cockamamie to us today. English standardization started in earnest with Noah Webster. In 1783, he published what he called a "speller," which was a precursor to the first *American Dictionary of the English Language*, which came out in 1828. Printers started standardizing for efficiency, and the ball was rolling.[3] And yet, here we are in the twenty-first century with nonstandard town names. WBSM radio reported on a Reddit thread where Massachusetts residents tried to explain to non-

Massachusetts residents what the boro/borough situation was about. Here are some of the funnier posts they reported:

> *"In North Attleborough you go to Dunkin' Doughnuts."*
> *"Ugh can be used. Or not. It's confusing. That's why it's 'ugh.'"*
> *"It's Massachusetts! All the spellings of cities/towns are screwed up!"*[4]

The boroughs are full of fantastic stories, just like the hams (chapter 18.) I could tell you all of them but that would have to be another (large) book. For now, here are a few quick stories and one meatier story.

The Oliver Estate

I researched this against my better judgment, because I am an absolute wuss when it comes to ghosts—an utter, complete wuss. But like anyone, and especially any New Englander, I can't avert my eyes. I have to know. Well, I wish I didn't know about the Oliver Estate, because it's creepy beyond all human belief. It was built in 1769 as a wedding gift for Peter Oliver and Sally Hutchinson. (Pretty sure I got salad tongs and a mixer for my wedding gift.) It's massive and gorgeous, of course, and sits on a big parcel of land. Before I get into the spooky stuff, let me say that the history of the Oliver house is wild. It played a huge role in the American Revolution and the Underground Railroad. I'm focusing on the ghosts here, but there is a lot more to the Oliver House story than just the supernatural.

Okay, so far prior to the Olivers' arrival, a Wompanoag tribe lived on the back part of the property, along the Nemasket River. The tribe was wiped out by disease when settlers started arriving in the early seventeenth century, and there were multiple burial mounds throughout the Olivers' property. Between the Native American history and the colonial history, it's hard to know the origins of the purported haunting, but either way, I won't be sleeping tonight.

In an interview with the Mercy College newspaper in 2020, the Oliver House's Chris Andrade told a story that makes me want to go hide under my bed with my wedding-gift salad tongs as a weapon.

> *I started walking through the huge closet to get back to the group of people....I looked to my left and there was this girl standing there in the*

> *same kind of dress I was in (colonial costume), with a bonnet on her head. I was like: "What the hell? Why is Christy* [the ghost tour manager] *hiding in the closet?"*

Her initial thought was that she was being pranked.

> *I looked at the girl again and I realized, "Oh my God, this isn't Christy!"…Her most prominent feature was her eyes. They were huge. It didn't look natural.*

It took Andrade a moment to realize that she had a bona fide apparition standing in front of her. She scanned through some options in her head before reacting. Had she announced to the group in the next room over what was standing in front of her, they would have either stormed the closet or pushed themselves down the stairs to get out of the house as fast as possible.

> *So, I didn't know what to do….In a split second, I looked back over at this girl, and just as quickly, she put her finger up to her lips as if to say: "Don't tell." She took one step backward and into the wall she disappeared.*

Andrade tore the closet apart searching for the chambermaid she had seen, but she was nowhere to be found. It took Andrade days to fully wrap her head around the experience and get confirmation that she wasn't going insane. "Christy just told me like a year ago: 'I knew you had seen something because you were different.'"[5]

Yeah, I'd be different too. Specifically, I would have freaked out so hard that I'd have to be put into a medically induced coma.

In 2022, Stephanie Forlini, a TikTok influencer who shares metaphysical videos and discusses paranormal topics, and Tim Weisberg of WBSM Radio spent the night in the house. Weinberg wrote an article for WBSM about the experience:

> *Throughout the night, we often heard footsteps and voices in other parts of the house, when we knew it was just the four of us, all in the same room, that were the only ones occupying the building.*
>
> *Just before 7:30 a.m. Saturday morning, the camera in the "Old Kitchen" of the house captured what appears to be the wooden bar sliding out of the iron holder, completely on its own, with a loud bang as the wood*

hits the floor. In the seconds following that, voices can be heard on the recording, although it's hard to make out what they are saying.

In an article in South Coast Today, Selectman Diane Stewart reported the following experience toward the end of a late-night Conservation Commission meeting:

The whole commission heard this screaming and singing alternately upstairs, and one of our members went up to check. There was nobody out there. So I would say that I am pretty solidly a skeptic in general but definitely heard some screaming and singing.[6]

If you need to be further terrified, the Oliver House regularly posts paranormal footage and audio to their Facebook page. Paranormal-focused events are also hosted regularly at the house. I will not be attending, neither with nor without defensive salad tongs at the ready.

PRAYING INDIAN TOWNS

Does the term *Praying Indian* make you uncomfortable? Good. It should. Praying Indian towns were established by missionaries in the seventeenth century to house Native Americans who had converted to Christianity. Some of these conversions were voluntary; some were not. Marlborough was the site of one of the main Praying Indian towns, Okommakamesit.[7] Okommakamesit was established in 1654 by minister John Eliot to

separate Native people from their traditional lifeways, spiritual traditions, and kinship networks so that they could work towards converting to the Puritan faith. Native people moved to praying towns for many reasons, including a desire for land security, economic survival, the possibility of English legal protection, and a curiosity about the Puritan faith during tremendous upheaval due to epidemics and English expansion.[8]

The village was occupied by about fifty members of the Pennacook tribe.

By 1674, Okommakamesit was one of fourteen Praying Indian towns, with around 1,100 inhabitants in total. That's just around the time that King Philip's War broke out, with Native American leader Metacomet allying several tribes to try to push the colonists out of their lands once and for all. While the Praying Indians of Okommakamesit had mostly moved to the 1660 settlement of Marlborough, they were not safe from what happened next. The colonists had taken the Praying Indians in as their own fellow Christians, until the war made them fearful of the Praying Indians switching sides and allying themselves with Metacomet. To avoid this, the colonists had all of them shipped out to what amounted to concentration camps on Deer Island in the Boston Harbor with only what they could carry. Some of the younger, stronger men were sold into slavery in the Caribbean as they were seen as the most likely to be able to escape the island. John Eliot fought against this and tried to defend those in his villages, but he was overwhelmed by public sentiment and could not stop the internment. When they were finally allowed off the island, many had died. Now, the colonists were wary of them because of their heritage, and their original tribes were wary of them because of their alliance with the English. Most of the women and children became indentured servants in English households, and the men were sold into slavery.[9] The Praying Indians had joined the towns to try to save themselves but were only able to delay the inevitable.

Tom Cook

The initial story I heard about Tom Cook was that he was born, he got sick, his mom said something that clergy interpreted as her offering his soul to the devil for him to be healthy and then he eventually outsmarted the devil when he came to collect and went on to be a thief. Meh. Every New England town has some version of that story. But Marlborough's is a lot cooler than that.

Tom Cook was born on October 6, 1738. He was happy, healthy and cute, and his mom adored him. Then, when he was three, he suddenly became sick. The clergy prayed over him, and he didn't get better. His mom was despondent and is said to have yelled out, "Only spare his life, only spare his life, and I care not what he becomes!"[10] As innocuous as that may sound to a modern-day ear, the pious of 1738 took it to mean Tom's mother was basically offering up his soul to the devil in exchange for him regaining his health. Feels like a stretch to me, but a lot has changed in two hundred years. Tom started to get better. Quickly, he was a healthy toddler again, which set puritanical tongues wagging all the more. Clearly the devil had taken Tom's mother up on her offer and restored the child's health in eventual exchange for his soul.

Tom continued to grow up and became a bit of a scamp. He was known for stealing and generally causing trouble around town. When he was thirteen, the devil came to him and reached out his hand. It was time to pay up. Tom was getting dressed when the devil called, and his quick wits presented him with a way out of descent into hell, or eternal servitude or whatever happens when the devil owns your soul. He said, "Will you wait a minute until I put my suspenders on?" to which the devil nodded his head. Tom took his suspenders and tossed them in the fire. Because the devil had agreed not to take him until his put on his suspenders, he was safe from the soul-taking pact as long as he never again wore them. He had successfully outsmarted the devil.[11]

Now Tom really amped up the stealing. He became a notorious thief—but a very specific type of thief. Tom would steal from rich people—their food, their livestock, wares from their shops—and give them to the poor people of the towns he passed through. Kind of like Robin Hood, right?

Wrong.

Because it's more likely that Robin Hood is kind of like Tom Cook. Well, sort of.

The Robin Hood legends start cropping up in England around the fifteenth century, but that Robin Hood was a malcontent who lived in Sherwood Forest and went around murdering landowners and aristocrats to right the wrongs of the crumbling feudal system. It wasn't until hundreds of years later that Robin Hood started "stealing from the rich to give to the poor" in the way we know. In fact, that transformation in the legend started happening not too long after Tom Cook's story began circulating. Some scholars believe that the story of the real-life Tom Cook, stealing from the rich to give to the poor, melded with that of the Sherwood Forest rebel. With the feudal system gone by then but with huge economic disparities still very real, it makes sense that the legend would morph, too.[12]

So what initially looked like a pretty straightforward colonial New England "this guy interacted with the devil" story ends up potentially having influence on a world-famous, very English, legend. Isn't history cool?

---

1. David Wade, "Boro or Borough: What's the Proper Spelling for Massachusetts Towns?," CBS Boston, March 31, 2023, https://www.cbsnews.com.
2. Ibid.

3. Eileen Holmes Pearson, "The Standardization of American English," Teaching History, https://teachinghistory.org.
4. Kate Robinson, "Is It Attleboro or Attleborough? Reddit Explains," 1420 WBSM, January 16, 2023, https://wbsm.com.
5. Francesca Simone, "Secrets of the Oliver House," *Impact*, December 22, 2020, https://theimpactnews.com.
6. Matthew Ferreira, "Paranormal Investigators Say Oliver Estate Is 'Extremely Haunted,'" *New Bedford Standard-Times*, October 29, 2015, https://www.southcoasttoday.com.
7. Native Northeast Portal, "Marlborough, Plymouth County, Massachusetts," https://nativenortheastportal.com.
8. Natick Historical Society, "Natick's Beginnings: Woodland Cultures, John Eliot and the 'Praying Indians,'" https://www.natickhistoricalsociety.org.
9. Boston Harbor Islands, "John Eliot: Father of 'Praying Villages,'" December 8, 2021, https://www.bostonharborislands.org.
10. Elizabeth Callahan, "The Legend of Tom Cook and the Devil," USC Digital Folklore Archives, May 16, 2012, https://folklore.usc.edu.
11. Westborough Library Local History, "Folktale Friday: Tom Cook (Forbes)," Westborough Center for History and Culture, July 5, 2019, https://www.westboroughcenter.org.
12. Jeff Belanger and Ray Auger, "Podcast 116: The Robin Hood of Massachusetts," New England Legends, https://ournewenglandlegends.com.

ABOUT THE AUTHOR

Amanda Rotondo is a storyteller who finds the funny and the fantastical in everyday situations. She has written articles and essays for various publications, as well as professional and academic book chapters and articles. She holds a PhD from Rensselaer and lives outside Boston with her family.